Beyond the Fringe

Researching a Spiritual Age

The report of Revd Yvonne Richmond's research in the Diocese of Coventry into the spirituality of people outside the Church

Nick Spencer

The London Institute for Contemporary Christianity

cliff
COLLEGE
PUBLISHING

ISBN 1 898362 34 3

**Cliff College Publishing,
Calver, Hope Valley, Derbyshire S32 3XG**

Printed by:

MOORLEY'S Print & Publishing
23 Park Rd., Ilkeston, Derbys DE7 5DA
Tel/Fax: (0115) 932 0643
using text supplied electronically

To God – to him be the glory – for bringing together this research and the many practical resources and projects already flowing from it.

Yvonne Richmond

Chaplain for Evangelism, Coventry Cathedral

Contents

Acknowledgements

Interviewers:

Mrs Rita Ashman, Mr Colin Briffa, Mrs Margaret East, Mrs Bridget Harper, Rev David Knight, Rev Kate Mier, Rev Keith Mobberley, Rev Yvonne Richmond, Miss Margaret Rose, Rev Frank Seldon and Rev Malcolm Tyler

Transcriptions:

Mrs Sue Williams

Funding:

Coventry Diocese's Forum for Parish Development and Evangelism

Springboard

Archbishops' Council of The Church of England

St John's Church, Kenilworth

The London Institute for Contemporary Christianity

The Group For Evangelisation (Churches Together in England)

Foreword
by the Right Reverend Colin Bennetts,
Bishop of Coventry

'Features of contemporary society make it possible to speak to the heart of the matter. Therefore with a proper confidence take soundings – listen to words of the prophet written on subway walls and read the signs of the times.'

So said Bishop Michael Marshall in his opening address at 'Travelling Light', Coventry Diocese's conference in March 1999. A great many of us went away from that conference invigorated, challenged, excited and yet a little perplexed. Invigorated, challenged and excited because we were discerning spiritual changes within our society, which speakers and workshops at the conference were helping us address Perplexed because we needed, somehow, to become bilingual, to speak the language of God and the language of contemporary society. But how were we to understand the signs of the times to which Bishop Michael had made reference? How could we listen to the words of the prophet from subway walls? Where was the point of reference and what kind of spirituality, if any, would we encounter if we were to engage with those outside the Church walls? Only two years earlier we had witnessed extraordinary scenes following the death of Princess Diana, which caused Brian Appleyard, a respected journalist writing for the Sunday Times, to say: ' .... *there can be no doubt that we are in the midst of a religious upsurge. What are these people at the shrines doing? They are reaching beyond the grave; praying for meaning.'* And if there was a religious upsurge, what did that mean? How were we in the church engaging with that?

Yvonne Richmond was one who had been grappling with these and similar questions for many years. Her story is told in *'Evangelism in a Spiritual Age: communicating faith in a changing culture'*, the Church House Publishing book that accompanies this report. Challenged still further by the work of David Hay and Kate Hunt at the University of Nottingham, and wanting to understand more of how the church might engage with those outside its walls, Yvonne in partnership with Nick Spencer, devised a research programme to explore those very issues. Coventry Diocese, and indeed the wider church, has much to be grateful for in *Beyond the Fringe*. The findings, whilst not certainly proving the religious upsurge asserted by Brian Appleyard, do demonstrate people's willingness to engage with the big questions and send a signal to us within the Church that, perhaps as never before, we really need to ensure that we communicate the relevance of our faith in a way that meets people starting from where they are.

Some of the respondents' answers might lead us to conclude that they are far from God and cause us to despair of ever locating a relevant point of communication. But that is to have limited vision. That people were willing to talk about big questions seems to me to indicate some stirring of the Spirit and perhaps we need to enter into what God is probably already doing in their lives, rather than telling God what we are going to do for him.

Jesus, of course, so amply modelled this when he met the woman at the well. Perhaps we have become immune to the fact that it was nothing short of scandalous for Jesus to drink from the well and cup of a Samaritan – and a woman at that! Perhaps we too need to give up cultural inhibitions, and if we are to get to a position where a thirsty world finds such water it will almost certainly be because we have been willing to move beyond the merely conventional into areas where we do not feel safe, into risky ventures of faith where there is no guaranteed return for our investment.

Beyond the Fringe is an important piece of research, which all of us should take seriously. It is part of the 'soundings' to which Bishop Michael made reference and, with discernment, should help us all to read the signs of the times and encourage us to follow God into risky ventures of faith for the furtherance of his Kingdom.

The Right Reverend Colin Bennetts,
Bishop of Coventry
November 2004

Accompanying Resources

1. <u>*Evangelism in a Spiritual Age: communicating faith in a changing culture*</u>   Steve Croft, Rob Frost, Mark Ireland, Anne Richards, Yvonne Richmond and Nick Spencer

   Church House Publishing, March 2005

   A theological and practical introduction to the evangelistic challenge presented by contemporary spirituality.

2. <u>*Equipping Your Church in a Spiritual Age,*</u> Steve Hollinghurst, Yvonne Richmond and Roger Whitehead with Janice Price and Tina Adams

   Produced by The Group for Evangelisation (Churches Together in England), March 2005

   A workbook for church councils to begin considering their practical engagement with contemporary spirituality.

3. <u>Evangelistic contact cards with accompanying posters and resources</u>, available from The Christian Enquiry Agency, 27 Tavistock Square, London WC1H 9HH tel: 020 7387 3659, email: cea@christianity.org.uk

4. www.churchinaspiritualage.org.uk
   <u>Website</u> for further information, ideas and resources.

Introduction

Is Britain post-Christian? It is a simple question, but the obvious simple answer, 'yes', obscures a complex and confusing reality. The Church has less influence on society and culture today than at almost any time in the last millennium. Hardly 1 in 12 people regularly attends church and the number of baptisms, confirmations, and church marriages has been in free fall for years.

Yet to many people's surprise, the 2001 Census reported that over 70% of people in England and Wales claimed that their religion was Christian.[2] Research for the British Social Attitudes survey in 1998 recorded that 72% of people described themselves as theists of some kind, whilst only 10% were openly atheist.[3] The BBC poll for the programme 'What the world thinks of God' reported that 3 in 4 people pray at some time.[4] Research for another BBC programme, 'The Soul of Britain', in 2000, recorded that 38% of people said they believed Jesus was the 'son of God', 51% said they believed in life after death, 32% the resurrection of the dead, 52% heaven and 28% hell.[5]

Squaring this circle is not particularly easy. One way of understanding this apparently contradictory evidence is to see the Christian skeleton, which has long held and structured

---

1   cf. Christian Research, Religious Trends (www.christian-research.org.uk/res.htm)
2   www.statistics.gov.uk/census2001/default.asp
3   Office for National Statistics, Social Trends 30 (www.statistics.gov.uk/StatBase/xsdataset.asp?vlnk=1451&Pos=&ColRank=1&Rank=272)
4   http://news.bbc.co.uk/1/hi/programmes/wtwtgod/default.stm
5   www.facingthechallenge.org/soul.htm

people's spiritual lives, as having decayed and left in its place a slowly unravelling and increasingly amorphous body of often powerfully-held spiritual beliefs, many of which are shaped by the ghost of Christian doctrine. Time and again research surveys have shown how 'spiritual' we are as a nation (although that is a word that is open to much interpretation) and how, despite the fact we have no interest in church or in 'organised religion', we still favour Christian ethics and identify with elements of Christian doctrine.

Surveys in 1987 and 2000 showed that the percentage of people reporting some kind of spiritual experience had increased universally in that period. The proportion of people detecting 'a patterning of events', an 'awareness of the presence of God', an 'awareness of prayer being answered', an 'awareness of a sacred presence in nature', an 'awareness of the presence of the dead', and an 'awareness of an evil presence' had increased in every instance. The overall percentage of people who claimed to have experienced any of these events rose from 48 to 76%.[6] According to MORI, 31% of people claim to believe in astrology, 38% in ghosts, 42% in telepathy, 40% in guardian angels, 54% in premonitions/ ESP, 57% in deja-vu, 32% in out of body experiences, 60% in near death experiences, 28% in psychics/ mediums and 24% in faith healers.[7]

Beyond the Fringe was intended to analyse this phenomenon in greater detail. Other research projects had explored this area (notably David Hay and Kate Hunt's study, *Understanding the spirituality of people who don't go to church*) and *Beyond the Fringe* set out to expand on this work and to relate it to

---

6   Figures quoted in David Hay and Kate Hunt, *Understanding the spirituality of people who don't go to church* (University of Nottingham, 2000)

7   http://www.mori.com/polls/2003/bbc-heavenandearth-top.shtml

people's everyday lives and concerns (the starting point of the interviews) and also to their attitude to Christianity, Christians and the Church.

As it emerged, one question proved pivotal to the entire project and it is this, and more specifically the range of answers to it, which has been used to structure this research report. That question, whether there was one big question of life to which interviewees wanted an answer, respondents' answers to it (which fell into six categories) and their subsequent, often tentative responses in those six areas, form the structure of section A of this report.

Section B examines respondents' attitudes to Christianity and the Church, and how Christian responses, in as far as they were understood, do or do not satisfy the questions people were asking. In doing so, this section touches on several earlier research projects, notably *Beyond Belief?* conducted by the London Institute for Contemporary Christianity in November 2002. This section examines opinions of Jesus, the Bible, heaven, hell and the Church, exploring the nature and reason for people's (mis)understanding of them and the impact this has on their spiritual quest.

The final section seeks briefly to link together the previous two sections and introduce the beginnings of a response to the vibrant if non-Christian spirituality described therein. It should be read alongside the other publications and resources listed below, that have roots in these research findings and have been developed to provide a more wide-ranging and practical response to our spiritual age.

Although the acknowledgements detail those people and organisations who have contributed to *Beyond the Fringe*, I would like to register my enormous debt of gratitude to

Yvonne Richmond and her team of volunteers who were at the heart of the entire project. *Beyond the Fringe* was Yvonne's vision and she deserves full credit not only for making it happen and keeping it on track but also for linking it to other ventures exploring the nature of spiritual, 'post-Christian' Britain. Her volunteers – Rita Ashman, Colin Briffa, Margaret East, Bridget Harper, David Knight, Kate Mier, Keith Mobberley, Margaret Rose, Frank Seldon and Malcolm Tyler – dedicated a great deal of time and energy in contacting and interviewing respondents, and Sue Williams spent hours on the thankless task of transcribing the interviews. Without them the entire project would not have been possible and they deserve full credit for having managed to explore such an interesting area so sensitively and successfully. I extend to them all my deepest thanks for their vision, efforts and commitment.

Nick Spencer
London, November 2004

Sample details and research process

A team of eleven interviewers conducted 60 one-to-one interviews. These were split roughly equally between students (aged over 16), pre-family individuals, people with early families (i.e. children of primary school age or younger), people with late families (i.e. children of secondary school age), empty nesters (people whose children had left home), and widow(er)s. There were slightly more female than male respondents and they lived in rural, outer city, inner city, and town environments. Around half had been to church as a child, and many had attended for weddings and funerals. The majority had been baptised as children. None was a regular church attender at the time of the interview.

Interviewers recruited respondents through existing networks (i.e. friends of friends of friends, etc). Some knew their respondents before the interview but the majority did not and in no case was the existing relationship close enough to have distorted the interview process.

Interviewers were open about their background and the research objectives. They used a research guide that had been developed in advance and that enabled respondents to open up and talk about issues they held dear. Interviewers steered respondents through the guide with sufficient flexibility so that respondents' concerns and interests were permitted to shape the interviews to an extent. Respondents were universally happy with the process and many expressed their enjoyment of the interviews.

All interviews were recorded and transcribed for the analysis process, although no names or contact details were included in the transcriptions.

Anyone wishing to try a similar interview themselves will find a slightly modified, photocopiable version of the *Beyond The Fringe* interview guide in the workbook *Equipping Your Church in a Spiritual Age.*

Executive Summary

- Every respondent, irrespective of his or her own personal beliefs, professed to having **big questions** to which they wanted answers, although the extent to which they were actively seeking answers differed greatly, with many reporting that the weight of daily life often prevented such reflection.

- These questions were, in approximate order of importance, about:

  o **Destiny**: What happens after we die? Where, if anywhere, are we going?

  o **Purpose**: What is the point of life? What values should I live by? Whose life and values should I take as an example to inspire me?

  o **The universe**: How did it start? Is it designed? Is it planned? Is it controlled in any way?

  o **God**: Does he/it exist? If so, what is he/it like? (Is God a 'he' or an 'it', for example?) What, if any, viable relationship could there be between God and human beings?

  o **The spiritual realm**: Is there a spiritual realm? What form does it take? Does it have any relevance to me and to my life?

  o **Suffering**: Why is there so much in the world? What national and international issues concern me? What can be done about them?

- Respondents' answers to these questions were varied and sometimes confused, and were often held tentatively or even unwittingly.

- The commonest form of **destiny** envisaged was a spiritualised, disembodied, reuniting kind of afterlife.
- Respondents did not claim that life has a **purpose** but lived as if it did, that purpose being either to 'seize the day' and make the most of one's life, or to live for other people and other causes, sacrificing ambitions for them; a tension that was not easily reconciled.
- Broadly speaking, **the universe** was seen as awesome, created, largely ordered, probably designed, perhaps guided and possibly planned. People's understanding was self-confessedly insufficient, deeply anthropocentric and usually hesitant.
- A small minority of respondents dismissed **God** out of hand. The majority that did not and professed some belief in him/it, did so very hesitantly. The God they envisaged was, on one hand, an abstract explanation for all there is, credible but remote and frankly irrelevant, and on the other, a personal 'being' (although by no means the loving father of the Bible) who was closer but rather less credible.
- Attitudes to the **spiritual realm** differed according to respondent and type of spiritual experience. Many experiences were readily dismissed, including tances, premonitions, visions, and out-of-body experiences, whereas others, including ghosts, miracles and angels were deemed more interesting (although respondents' understanding of them was often secularised or highly figurative.)
- Respondents had a powerful sense that something was wrong with the world, a fact that was more obvious in concrete discussions about real personal, social and international problems than in abstract discussions of **suffering**. Although that suffering did implicate 'God', specific discussions also pointed the finger at a multitude

of more earthly causes, including global capitalism, liberal do-gooders and religious fanatics.

- There was no obvious link between the questions people were asking and the answers **Christianity** was perceived to offer, although this is not entirely surprising given the recruitment criteria for respondents.

- **Jesus** emerged from interviews with a good reputation although enfeebled by being seen, by many respondents, as a great teacher rather than divine in any sense. Among human beings, he was considered one of the best, living and dying for love, wisdom and other people. As every age has a tendency to remodel Jesus in its own image, so *Beyond the Fringe* respondents unconsciously shaped him in the image of their age. Thus Jesus became a human being touched by spiritual wisdom, a teacher, an 'individual', and a courageous rebel, whose life was brutally cut down by one set of institutional authorities and then systematically misrepresented by another.

- The **Bible**, in as far as it symbolised traditional, institutional religion, was commonly dismissed, on the basis it was unreliable, self-contradictory or malign. Having said that, once it had been neutered – by being treated as 'just' a story, a series of metaphors, moral education for children, or some such safe formula – it could be recognised and even praised. A deconstructed Bible, which allowed people to pick and choose, and which made few (or preferably no) demands on them, was an acceptable Bible.

- **Heaven** was, not surprisingly, an attractive concept to respondents, although in as far as it could be envisaged, it was a thoroughly spiritualised, Platonic heaven of disembodied souls.

- **Hell** was, not surprisingly, a less popular idea, although useful as a concept and cited, albeit very hesitantly and indirectly, by those respondents who talked about serious moral wickedness. It was an abominable prospect but not necessarily more objectionable than rape or child abuse.

- All the usual criticisms (and abuse) were levelled at **the Church** (dull, narrow, bigoted, hypocritical, embarrassing, unreal, prescriptive, unspiritual, judgmental, etc), although these were tempered by some favourable experiences and more positive attitudes. The single most important criticism levelled at it was that it was unnecessary. As one respondent remarked, *'I don't need the church because I have got God anyway'.*

- Overall, there was a **disconnection** between the big questions people had and (their perception of) Christianity's traditional responses. This had as much to do with respondents' ignorance and prejudice as ecclesiastical failings, but points towards the important need to articulate and embody the *relevance* of the Christian faith, whether that be through employing language that connects with rather than alienates people; developing worship and liturgy that inspire rather than bemuse participants; telling stories that enthuse rather than bore listeners; offering advice and practical workshops that make a genuine difference to people's lives; providing a protected arena in which people can operate as human beings rather than consumers; or simply offering a place of stillness and depth in which people are encouraged to reflect on the big questions that are so often buried under the frenetic routines of their lives.

Section A
What are the questions?

One Big Question

If there were one question you could have answered, what would it be? This was the question that every respondent faced at some point during his or her *Beyond the Fringe* interview.

The answers given were instructive and help to outline the building blocks of contemporary spirituality in the words and categories of the interviewees themselves. For this reason they have been used to structure the first part of this report and may, in turn, be used to guide the Church's mission in contemporary Britain.

The fact that so many (i.e. all) respondents had 'big questions', even, it should be noted, those who were openly and determinedly atheistic, naturalistic and materialist, is in itself important. It is fashionable today to claim than humans are 'just animals', a trend illustrated by a number of respondents and encouraged by the recent mapping of the human genome and the seemingly relentless march of neo-Darwinism over recent years. The presence of these stubborn 'metaphysical' questions and the tentative answers to them serve as a reminder of what makes humans peculiar and distinctive.

If we share 98% of our genes with chimpanzees, it has been asked, are we any more than 2% 'distinctive'? A comprehensive answer to this question is, of course, beyond the scope of this report, but respondents' big questions and their answers to them do at least point towards a response.

First, we are uniquely **question-asking** creatures. No respondent hesitated at the idea of having one big question they wanted answered, although several were unable to restrict themselves to only one. The questions themselves differed but nobody claimed that the idea of having a big question was meaningless or self-delusional. Although the word itself was (understandably) absent from respondents' lips, the research made it abundantly clear that if we are monkeys, we are monkeys with a peculiar interest in*metaphysics*.

Second, we are **destiny-**driven animals. In some form, 'what happens after we die?' was the single most common big question asked.

I suppose I'd like to know what does happen when you die. (Interview 1: Female, Student, Rural)

The big question would be "Is there life after death?" really. (Interview 37: Male, Student, Suburban Town)

Is there an afterlife? (Interview 44: Male, Pre-Family, Suburban Town)

The question of destiny was not restricted to those who had convinced themselves that there was an 'afterlife' but interested those who claimed to believe that we simply rotted away in the ground.

What happens when we die? Or why are we here? But in a way I wouldn't ask why are we here because I believe in evolution that is how it happened. Therefore it would be nice to know what happens after we die because then you can start to feel a bit more confident about it. (Interview 51: Female, Early Family, Suburban City)

It is worth noting, in passing, the mention of 'evolution' in this young woman's comment, a topic that came up with some frequency in interviews. The word is used, here and elsewhere, not as an *argument* against metaphysics or teleology but as a kind of magic spell to dissolve alternatives and explain the world. 'Evolution' is a kind of scientific 'abracadabra' to make difficult questions disappear.

Third, we are **purpose**-driven animals. Again in slightly different forms, the question, 'why am I here?' appeared regularly. Although a tiny handful of respondents rejected this question on the basis that they assumed 'evolution' made it nonsensical, the vast majority (among them many firm 'believers' in evolution) thought otherwise.

People have always got that thing in the back if their heads as to 'Why we are here?'. There must be a reason. I don't care whether people say they don't believe in God or whatever. They have still got that thought in the back of their head. It is instinctive in everyone. (Interview 49: Male, Student, Suburban City)

What is the meaning of life? Why are we here? We are here to serve a purpose but what is that purpose? (Interview 2: Male, Pre-Family, Rural)

Closely linked to the question of purpose was that of morality. As (only) one or two respondents explicitly remarked, the question of human destiny is linked to that of human morality.

No, [I have] three [questions]. The big question about why am I here. I would like to have a better understanding of life and I am very intrigued about good and evil. (Interview 35: Female, Empty Nester, Suburban Town)

Fourth, we are creatures acutely conscious of the**universe** and our place within it. Questions about the universe, its origins, size and meaning made up a sizeable minority of respondents' 'big questions'.

I would like to know how did it all start. (Interview 40: Male, Late Family, Suburban Town)

How big is the universe? Where does it end and where does it finish?... How do I know that there is not something out there that is huge looking down on me? (Interview 47: Male, Empty Nester, Suburban Town)

A subset of this question was the interest in alien life, itself related to the issue of human uniqueness and thereby human purpose.

I would love to know about things from outer space like aliens, God and the devil and heaven and hell. I don't see where they can be. (Interview 43: Female, Student, Suburban Town)

If there is any life anywhere else in this non-ending universe. (Interview 52: Female, Late Family, Suburban City)

Fifth, we are creatures with a nagging awareness of and interest in some higher power, usually but not always called **God**. This is not to say that the question 'isthere a God?' was paramount to respondents, let alone to claim that people's lives were consumed by the quest for God. Instead, God was often considered as an adjunct to the big questions of destiny and purpose.

What is the meaning of life or does God exist or is this all there is?... For myself it is I am here to serve a particular purpose and I feel that my life is predestined – will I be happy? (Interview 27: Female, Early/ Late Family, Urban City)

It is within this category that openly 'spiritual' questions were asked, about the **spiritual realm**, although this term could be used with considerable vagueness, and might be treated as a synonym for God or higher power.

What is it this spiritual essence that I have been searching and trying to understand? (Interview 61: Female, Late Family/ Empty Nester, Urban City)

Sixth, we are aware of **suffering**, that something is wrong with the world. Once again the various formulas for expressing this concern varied but even taking into account respondents' propensity to bemoan the state of the world today, most expressed genuine disquiet, either with straightforward social reasons or with a more theological interest.

Why is there so much suffering in the world? (Interview 21: Female, Early Family, Urban City)

Why is there so much injustice in the world? Where was God? (Interview 11: Male, Empty Nester, Rural)

These six factors – our inherent question-asking nature, our concern with destiny, purpose, the universe, God and 'spirituality', and suffering – are all distinctly human characteristics. We may have a great deal in common with chimpanzees but it seems unlikely that they lie awake at night contemplating the starry firmament or worried about their eternal destiny.

The point may sound trite but it is important, particularly given the inclination of many respondents to describe humans as *only* animals (even when they don't follow up the implications of that self-description). The main body of this research report explores the nature of these spiritual concerns and then examines the Church's response to them but it is important not to lose sight of the fundamental fact that allows us to engage in that analysis in the first place. It may, as respondents stated, be difficult to believe in humans relating to God (even if one believes in God) but given the peculiar characteristics of human beings it is all the more difficult to believe that they are *no more than* upright apes.

1. Questions about Destiny

Of all the 'big questions' mentioned by respondents, that of destiny was most straightforward, usually taking the form 'What happens after we die?'

Answers to the question were less straightforward, the research revealing a very wide spectrum of opinions.

At one end of the spectrum were those who said 'nothing' and were quite open about the prospect of rotting in the ground. Reasons for this opinion were themselves varied. On one account it was because humans are essentially animals, purely biological beings with no 'soul', the implication being that you had to have a non-material soul in order to survive death.

I just see us as biological beings and what happens to us is the same as what happens to any other animal. (Interview 43: Female, Student, Suburban Town)

The common sense side of me says that we get buried or burnt these days. Our body would naturally go into the ground as fertiliser. (Interview 56: Male, Early Family, Suburban City)

As already noted, the concept of evolution was cited as a (self-evident) explanation of this.

It sends a shiver and I can't dwell on it very long because I don't like to think that that is it. I believe in evolution, so I think that's it. (Interview 51: Female, Early Family, Suburban City)

For some the necessary proof was to be found in the fact that no-one had ever come back to tell them. If therewas life after death someone would have come back to say so.

Absolutely nothing [happens]… If anyone could have come back my dad would have because he enjoyed life so much. (Interview 29: Female, Empty Nester, Urban City)

Some softened the enormity of this view by consoling themselves that, as the poet Philip Larkin wrote, 'no rational being/ Can fear a thing it will not feel'.[1]

I don't think anything happens after we die. In terms of first person consciousness, we will not be able to perceive that we are dead. That is not to say that our actions don't echo into eternity, but we are not conscious of them. (Interview 44: Male, Pre-Family, Suburban Town)

Of these 'nihilists' two incidental points can be made. Firstly, even those respondents who were most open about the prospect of annihilation admitted that they would prefer if it were otherwise; not for them the blessed release of death.

I would like to believe that we live on and go to this garden in the sky which is lovely, but I think it is a bit far fetched to be honest. I think you just either rot in a hole in the ground or your ashes get blown away by the wind. (Interview 21: Female, Early Family, Urban City)

Secondly, there was an interesting inverse correlation (using the word indicatively rather than statistically) between 'nihilism' and considered thought about death. By their own admission, those who expressed the 'rot in the ground' opinion had not thought about (let alone dwelt on) death very much.

I think we rot in the ground and that is it I am afraid. I am not worried about saying that but I probably will be when I am

---

1   *Aubade*, Philip Larkin

going to die. [Interviewer: Do you ever think about death?]
No, never. (Interview 7: Female, Student, Rural)

I don't believe in life after death. Once you are dead that is it,
gone, finished. [Interviewer: Do you ever think about death?]
No, not really. (Interview 16: Male, Late Family, Rural)

If the 'nihilistic' answers were relatively homogeneous, the
positive ones were quite the opposite. A far greater proportion
of the overall sample admitted to believing that there was *some*
existence after death although there was huge variety within
this general affirmation.

By far the largest 'yes' category favoured a vague, spiritual,
quasi-Platonic, peaceful, non-judgemental afterlife in which
one was reunited with friends and loved ones. First, the
physical body would be jettisoned, unneeded, and then one's
soul would soar.

I think you leave your physical body behind as you don't need
that anymore. (Interview 8: Female, Pre-Family, Rural)

I'd like to think that your spirit will be a free spirit and all you
are doing is laying your body to rest and there is another sort
of world – something else out there that your spirit will go to.
(Interview 2: Male, Pre-Family, Rural)

The whole experience was – or at least could be – marked by a
sense of freedom and a sense of peace.

I don't like to think that you just 'go'. I don't believe that… I
think you probably find peace. If you could honestly say you
have died and to your knowledge you have done the best you
can then I think you will probably have a peaceful time.
(Interview 45: Female, Early Family, Suburban Town)

Reunification with relatives would play a vital role.

It is nice to think that you would go and see all your family again and I think that you probably do. I don't think there is a place where some people go. I think everybody goes to the same place. I don't think people are judged in that sense. (Interview 45: Female, Early Family, Suburban Town)

You might be given the opportunity to view your life.

You are taken up by the angel of death as I see it. Depending on how open or previously knowledgeable you are, you then have the opportunity to review the whole of your life to see how well you have done. (Interview 8: Female, Pre-Family, Rural)

Or you might be allowed to take up a guardian-angel role yourself.

Hopefully you go to heaven and you can watch over and look after the people you love. (Interview 20: Female, Pre-Family, Urban City)

A handful of respondents claimed to believe this because of actual experiences (though not, noticeably, of dying), but they admitted this in itself was insufficient proof.

I have had a few weird experiences with regard to ghosts and things like that, but I would really like to know what there is and I definitely believe and hope that there is something after we die. (Interview 15: Female, Early Family, Rural)

I am certain we are going up there to another place, paradise. I get my mum and dad [to] come down and sit with me most nights and my wife. They always come to me in my dreams and we have a lovely conversation. (Interview 42: Male, Widowed, Suburban Town)

Some people had rather well developed belief systems based on this.

I also think you are met by other loved ones who are already on the other side and it is very joyful and you can have a rest for as long as you want before you incarnate again. It is sad because you can become what is called a trapped soul. If you believe all there is is the earth then you hang around in your old environment – that is what ghosts are. Another reason for hanging around is if you die in trauma, like in battle, you get trapped souls hanging around battlefields. (Interview 8: Female, Pre-Family, Rural)

Some even cited biblical justification for their beliefs.

I feel we go onto another dimension. I think that there are lots of dimensions as it says in the Bible. 'In my father's house there are many mansions.' Well, I put them down to dimensions. (Interview 58: Female, Late Family, Suburban City)

There were, of course, problems with this whole arrangement, such as *where* souls went and whether there would be sufficient room there. As far as people could tell it all happened in 'another dimension' or 'a different world'.

I believe that the spirit goes on and lives on in a different place and a different dimension but I believe it goes on whether you go into reincarnation or go on to some kind of better place. Essentially, I believe that the spirit does live on – as to where I couldn't tell you. (Interview 27: Female, Early/Late Family, Urban City)

For some, there was a serious space problem.

My daughter says we can't all go to heaven because there wouldn't be enough room. I said, 'No, it isn't like that.' Our soul goes to heaven and then it goes to somewhere else, that is what I think. (Interview 30: Female, Separated, Urban City)

These visions of the beyond made up the majority of after-life beliefs, but there were other, often stranger beliefs, some of which were quite difficult to understand. One respondent voiced her belief that *'there is no death as far as I am concerned' (Interview 8: Female, Pre-Family, Rural)*, although what she meant by that was unclear. Another young respondent claimed to believe in a kind of assimilation into oneness, in a belief that sounded vaguely eastern.

I believe that there is an ultimate being if you like or a oneness. I think we are all part of that oneness, or a whole. When the time is right and we have developed and found out who we are then basically we return to the whole. It is quite a deep concept to grasp. (Interview 49: Male, Student, Suburban City)

Another student, in a curious echo of the 'death doesn't really exist' response above, explained how he didn't think death existed because we were all essentially recycled energy.

From my point of view death doesn't really exist, because I believe everybody is energy, and whatever you do in life you can never get rid of energy, it always gets converted into something else. From my point of view, death to me is just another part of recycling. (Interview 49: Male, Student, Suburban City)

Reincarnation was mentioned in a few cases, but uncertainly and unconvincingly, and could easily be combined with more traditional (if thoroughly non-biblical) Christian views of death and judgement, as this long but fascinating quotation illustrates.

I think that I am not the first incarnation of myself. I think when I die my body will rot because it is designed to do that and will probably make some bloody good compost somewhere. I think my spirit will live on maybe in another form. I have read books about the afterlife. I am not dubious about it but I am not 1000% sure that you go along a nice bright tunnel and when you come to the end of it there is St Peter who says "Well you have done this or that.... so you can come in". I would like to think that it does. A place for the good people and a place for the really bad and evil people. They are not the same place and you do not get treated the same. That sounds rubbish and that you are going down the root of segregation but I don't want to be sharing my paradise when I move on into the next world with someone who thought it was good to kill six million Jewish people, or a rapist. I don't want to share my paradise. There is a place for good people and a place for bad people. (Interview 26: Male, Pre-Family, Urban City)

Such confusion was quite typical with some answers moving through various different belief systems and one or two regrettably incomprehensible under the weight of clever-sounding psychobabble. Again the following quotation is long but interesting in showing the way science, theology, philosophy and physiology could be combined in a single vision. It is also interesting for the respondent's tone of 'high seriousness' throughout.

It seems to me that each of us is a point of consciousness. I don't talk about the soul because I don't see any distinction. I am I. The point of consciousness can't experience its own non-existence, so the point in which you die, the point where the physical support mechanism for that point of consciousness ceases to function, something strange must happen to that point of consciousness. An analogy might be what happens when someone falls into a black hole in broad physics. It is something that happens there and then and you cease to exist in time and I don't know what happens ... I have a suspicion and it is only a suspicion that from the point of view of your own experience you do [continue to exist]. Now what form that existence takes I don't know. You read about near death experiences and talk about seeing ghosts and I have never had such an experience myself but people have. You can postulate that because you have existed in time and space and therefore our past is unchangeable, that is fixed. In some sense the self at a point of consciousness can continue to exist within that. The whole reason why the universe exists in the first place is to provide a means by which consciousness can exist. We are the means by which the universe experiences itself. (Interview 34: Male, Late Family, Suburban Town)

Given the detailed and sometimes convoluted personal metaphysical systems created by some respondents, it was not surprising that there were responses of plain confusion and uncertainty. In spite (or perhaps because) of this uncertainty, however, there was also, for some respondents at least, a powerful and moving desire to believe.

I would like to think I would go to heaven. I don't know exactly what would happen to me but I would hope that I would go somewhere nice. (Interview 59: Female, Empty Nester, Suburban City)

I am scared because we don't know... You see that is what I would like; a faith to believe that this is going to happen. But I can't get that faith and it doesn't matter how many books I read I cannot get that faith in here [points to head] or in here [points to heart].' (Interview 17: Female, Empty Nester, Rural)

I do believe in an afterlife for everybody else, but when it comes to me I am not sure. (Interview 52: Female, Late Family, Suburban City)

For some, caught on the horns of this dilemma, an afterlife, incredible as it may seem, was less incredible than the chances of there being nothing after death.

I believe we are too complex and we've got too much about us and we've got a soul to us. I can't imagine that we go through life and then we die and that is it. (Interview 32: Female, Pre-Family, Suburban Town)

As will be clear from the above comments, this (and indeed any) kind of belief in an afterlife was far more common among female respondents, with male ones being far more circumspect about their beliefs and more willing to face the possibility of extinction (though there seemed a touch of male bravado in this).

It is also worth noting that more exotic beliefs came from younger respondents, who, albeit unconsciously, mixed and mingled various different traditions in sometimes quite confusing ways. Conversely, and not surprisingly, older respondents were more 'orthodox' in their beliefs, although this term is used loosely. No respondent voiced anything like the Christian concept of the resurrection (a word conspicuous in its absence) and the presupposition was that the Christian vision of the afterlife was similar to the spiritual, Platonic one discussed above.

Judgement was an unpopular and uncomfortable subject and rarely mentioned in visions of the beyond. When it was mentioned, it tended to be by older respondents who themselves demonstrated a smorgasbord of beliefs, if one with slightly less exotic ingredients. Hence, from one older man, came this interesting (and charming) explanation.

I am not the best church attender but have you [addressing the interviewer] ever come to me to ask me to do anything for the church that I haven't done straight away? I decorate the church, get the Christmas tree, I will do anything. I cannot bring myself to believe in the hereafter and I don't think we have the right to. I live my life and have given more people a drink of water than I have kicked them on the ground and that is the way I look at it. I have done one or two things that I am not proud of, mostly out of ignorance, and I am ashamed to say, occasionally out of spite. So if there is a hereafter and it is based on how good you have been in life, I am not going to be terribly luxuriously accommodated, but I don't think I am going to be shovelling coal. (Interview 11: Male, Empty Nester, Rural)

It is also worth noting, in concluding this section, that not one single respondent claimed that the question about destiny was foolish. Even among the small minority who quickly dismissed it with a nihilistic sweep of the hand, there was often a desire for something more, though many admitted they shied away from the thought of death as far as possible. The destiny question is written into our very being.

2. Questions about Purpose

The question of purpose was less straightforward than that of destiny, having two distinct 'areas' of response: the purpose of the universe and the purpose of life. The former of these is addressed in the section on the universe below, the latter here.

Assessing the perceived purpose of life had its subtleties too, however. Whilst the question of destiny could be reasonably well encapsulated in the 'after death' discussion, that of purpose incorporated a number of distinct elements, metaphysical, moral and personal.

Respondents were therefore asked the overall question from a number of angles, both directly and indirectly: 'What sort of things matter to you?', 'Whom do you admire?', 'What would you say was important in life?', 'What would you like people to say about you on your 70th birthday?', and 'Do you feel the way you live will make any difference ultimately?'

Although the last of these might seem to be the most fruitful path to take in addressing the overall 'What are you here for?' question (itself too confrontational to be asked directly), it too tends to be too direct, with respondents unwilling to claim any great purpose for their lives and so falling back into self-deprecating humility.

Not to me, but my life may have had an influence on other people. (Interview 43: Female, Student, Suburban Town)

I would love to think it would [have a purpose] , and I keep hoping it will, but in reality my head says 'No, it won't', but that doesn't stop me trying to live in a good and proper way. (Interview 47: Male, Empty Nester, Suburban Town)

Instead the indirect questions about who and what are deemed to be most important in life proved better ways to access people's hidden sense of purpose. It was the answers to these questions that began to reveal a tension that ran through people's idea of their purpose.

The tension was caused by two distinct factors that shaped respondents' lives and objectives. The first was the belief, strongest among young respondents, that their purpose in life was to achieve as much as they could for themselves. Although this may sound nakedly selfish, it was not meant to. Rather it was the natural concomitant of a 'here-is-all-we-have', seize-the-day mentality.

At its most extreme, life was about *'doing what you want, being happy.' (Interview 1: Female, Student, Rural)*

The first thing that really matters to me is myself, definitely. How I feel about something. (Interview 49: Male, Student, Suburban City)

More precisely, it was the desire to get the most out of life or to fulfil one's potential.

Being happy and getting out of life what you want to get out of life because life is quite short really. (Interview 45: Female, Early Family, Suburban Town)

Enjoying life basically to its full and fulfilling your potential if possible... You've just got to get on and sort of really fulfil it as much as you can. (Interview 2: Male, Pre-Family, Rural)

This was reflected in a number of answers given to the request for a suitable 70th birthday accolade, again with younger respondents being more focused on themselves.

He lived to his potential, I guess, whatever that may be. (Interview 44: Male, Pre-Family, Suburban Town)

That I had never missed an opportunity to do what I think was right. I always enjoyed myself. (Interview 9: Female, Early Family, Rural)

She has achieved what she set out to do so far. (Interview 8: Female, Pre-Family, Rural)

Accordingly, independence and autonomy were hailed as particularly important qualities. Social pressure or indeed anything that prevented you from achieving your potential was an evil.

That I've lived how I've wanted to live. I've not been pressurised into doing anything I've not wanted to do. (Interview 1: Female, Student, Rural)

For some respondents (again, more often younger ones), this belief that we are here to aim for 'self-actualisation' (to use Abraham Maslow's famous phrase) was also evident in their answers to the question 'who they admired most'.

People who achieve their goals. (Interview 3: Male, Early Family, Rural)

Anyone who is prepared to do what makes them happy, to not compromise that conviction. (Interview 9: Female, Early Family, Rural)

However, for a greater proportion of respondents this was one point at which the tension at the heart of their sense of purpose began to show itself. People recognised that by its very nature self-actualisation demanded a concentration on oneself and one's potential. This needn't be in an aggressive or blatantly selfish way but it did mean pursuing *my* dreams and *my* potential.

It slowly became clear, however, that the quality most respected in life was self-sacrifice and the people most admired were those who were self-sacrificial. Relatives were of course, paramount in this respect but in a more public sphere people recognised that their heroes exhibited not just courage and conviction but also lived for a cause for which they were prepared to sacrifice themselves. Among the most frequently admired people were Nelson Mandela, Mother Theresa, Martin Luther King, Gandhi, and Jesus.

I admire people who stand out and stand away from things. Martin Luther King is a wonderful example, and I think the highest credit to him because he stood out and said what he felt. (Interview 37: Male, Student, Suburban Town)

People who make a big difference in life. Like Jesus himself... people who are prepared to die for their principles. (Interview 10: Male, Late Family, Rural)

Nor was this phenomenon limited to the great and the good. Indeed, it was more evident in everyday life and aspirations. Admired people needn't have a name.

I admire those people who go out to third world countries and give their all to help. (Interview 60: Male, Widowed, Suburban City)

When it came to qualities that were admired, self-fulfilment was dwarfed by the number of self-sacrificial and relational virtues mentioned by interviewees: 'respect...relationships...a caring attitude to people regardless... self-dignity... honesty... compassion... [and] patience'.

In much the same way, a 'good person' tended not to be someone who had achieved everything they wanted in life but rather someone who was 'honest... trustworthy... helpful... considerate... caring... kind... sharing... compassionate... strives to do the right thing... understanding... self-sacrificial... open-minded... committed.. [and] selfless.'

This resulted in a fundamental tension in people's sense of purpose, one that was most acute among young respondents. On the one hand, we are here to achieve our goals and a successful life is one in which circumstances have been overcome and dreams realised. On the other hand, the people and qualities I admire most are those where such ambitions are sacrificed for the good of other people. The best qualities in life were love and empathy. The best influences were those people who had put my needs before their own.

Love is extremely important because it gives you security and it gives you the security in which to be who you... to be the person that you are I think. Loyalty and security... I mean more emotional security. Because I think if you have that you have got a firm rock to stand on. It brings out a deeper level to you, to be more open. (Interview 32: Female, Pre-Family, Suburban Town)

The most popular 70th birthday tribute was the accolade of having been there for others. People wanted to be remembered not for what they achieved for themselves but for what they achieved for others.

I was a good friend, just that I was there when they needed me. (Interview 50: Female, Pre-Family, Suburban City)

Good chap, always delivered, always did the job, faithful, loyal, good friend, that sort of thing. (Interview 5: Male, Empty Nester, Rural)

And, predictably, it was disrespect, ingratitude and selfishness that most angered people.

When I see people who take advantage of things and basically couldn't give a damn... you hear it as well in their attitudes, "Why should I go out to work, I get it handed to me." (Interview 21: Female, Early Family, Urban City)

People do things and don't think how they impact on other people. I think there is too much of this 'just do what you want to do because you want to do it' without thinking about how that will impact on other people's lives. (Interview 22: Female, Late Family, Urban City)

This, then, was the tension that ran through people's sense of purpose. For many, particularly younger respondents, their sense of purpose was directed by themselves for themselves; yet, at the same time, it was also shaped by an admiration for those people who did just the opposite and were prepared to sacrifice their goals and themselves for other people.

The problem existed but in a slightly less pronounced form for older respondents, for whom the attractions of 'self-actualisation' were diminished and who had also, in many if not all circumstances, had children and recognised the importance of self-sacrifice first hand. Yet it remained a tension for many of these interviewees too.

2.1 The Moral Animal

It is worth noting, if only briefly, how this tension related to people's general moral outlook.

'Goodness', as exhibited by respondents' heroes, was widely applauded. No respondent professed a selfish or brutally social-Darwinian ethic or argued with the premise of the question 'why is it important to be good?'

Yet the reasons offered for the universal belief in the importance of goodness were interesting for their variety and their potential fragility. There was a subtle and often only implicit sense of the contingency rather than the necessity of morality. It was important to be good because of the benefits of goodness rather than because being good was in any way commanded or ordered, either by a creator or by the created order. At its most contingent, goodness was a function of personal happiness,

I prefer to be good because it makes me feel happier. (Interview 38: Male, Pre-Family, Suburban Town)

or of peace of mind.

If you were bad what peace have you got? (Interview 30: Female, Separated, Urban City)

Inner peace. If you feel good on the inside you will feel good on the outside and sleep well. (Interview 3: Male, Early Family, Rural)

Only a tiny handful of respondents remarked on the fact that it doesn't always work that way. Being good in order to feel good was a notoriously fragile state of affairs.

[There is the argument that] you are at more peace with yourself but that is not always true is it? Take a young lad who is going out and vandalising everywhere. He gets a great kick out of that, so for him that is good. (Interview 52: Female, Late Family, Suburban City)

Beyond reasons of personal happiness and peace of mind there were those of calculated self-interest.

If you are good you don't get into any trouble do you? (Interview 48: Female, Widowed, Suburban Town)

Some respondents thought in broader terms. Goodness became a social necessity. Being good made life better for everyone.

If everyone was good, society would be a lot better. (Interview 40: Male, Late Family, Suburban Town)

Life in general would be a lot easier... problems in general would get solved a lot quicker. (Interview 2: Male, Pre-Family, Rural)

Because it leads to happiness and prosperity for all. (Interview 8: Female, Pre-Family, Rural)

Finally there were the 'inverse-reasons'. Put simply, the alternative is worse.

Because if there weren't there would be arguments and wars going on even more so than there are now. (Interview 43: Female, Student, Suburban Town)

If you are not, the world will become an increasingly unpleasant place to be. (Interview 9: Female, Early Family, Rural)

Each of these reasons is, of course, true – to some degree. Immoral behaviour *does* trouble minds – until, that is, we redefine morality and anaesthetise our consciences. Immoral behaviour *does* destabilise society – although it needn't have any negative effect on the anti-social individual, or indeed on third parties who, in a wealthy, technological and individualised society are well able to isolate themselves from its effects. Uncertainty about the centrality or significance of morality in our lives and purpose had bred a subjectivism that, whilst not wrong, rather weakened any sense of the moral *imperative*.

Respondents were also asked whether they believed there were moral absolutes, although not in such terms, the question usually being phrased, 'Are there things which are always right or wrong?'

Responses again covered a spectrum of opinion from the 'No, everything is relative' answer to the 'Yes, there certainly are' response. Importantly, examples of shallow and subtle thinking were to be found at both ends of the spectrum.

Shallow examples of relativism abounded. For some people, just because one man's meat is another's poison, there was no such thing as absolute (an interesting example of what can happen when morality is made wholly contingent on human feelings).

I suppose like the obvious things like stealing, murder and drugs will always be wrong, but for some people they can only see them as right... it is an individual thing, every individual is different. I could tell you things that I think are right and wrong and then you could ask someone else and they would say the opposite... I don't think it is as much to do with the law as to how you feel. (Interview 21: Female, Early Family, Urban City)

Sometimes such relativism was as a result of our modern tolerance imperative.

You have got to be tolerant and in that point of view you have to accept the shades of grey. None of us are perfect, nobody is... that is life. (Interview 45: Female, Early Family, Suburban Town)

Very occasionally, someone would take their relativism to its (logical?) conclusion.

I don't believe there is such a thing as right or wrong. I think there is nothing you can do that is wrong. I mean you go to the extremities of like murdering somebody or stealing, but I believe everything happens for a reason. (Interview 49: Male, Student, Suburban City)

Other respondents held similar relativist views but had slightly more nuanced explanations, usually revolving around the importance of recognising a situation's particularities and extenuating circumstances.

No — I think in every circumstance you have to look at each thing individually. There are so many different situations where something normally wrong could be right. (Interview 1: Female, Student, Rural)

I think there are always going to be situations where things are going to be extreme and that aren't black and white. Even situations of murder, there can sometimes be extenuating circumstances. (Interview 45: Female, Early Family, Suburban Town)

At the other end of the spectrum, there were (roughly similar numbers of) people who said they thought certain aspects of morality were absolute. Nobody, it should be noted, was an out-and-out absolutist, claiming that there were no genuine moral debates to be had because everything was straightforward. On the contrary 'black and white' was almost a term of abuse, used to describe those incapable of serious moral thought.

Interestingly, very few of those at this end of the spectrum reckoned the taking of human life to be 'always wrong'. A number began in this vein but reconsidered their opinions in the light of further considerations.

I was going to say murder, but I am not sure what I think about euthanasia. (Interview 35: Female, Empty Nester, Suburban Town)

Taking a life I would say, but having said that it depends on whether it was self-defence. (Interview 38: Male, Pre-Family, Suburban Town)

Far more common was the perceived absolute prohibition of *abusing* a human life.

No one should have such power over someone else to make them completely helpless. Whether that is verbal torture, mental or physical it is equally damaging sometimes. (Interview 32: Female, Pre-Family, Suburban Town)

Nowhere was this more pronounced than in attitudes towards children. Child-abuse and rape were the most frequently mentioned moral absolutes, for which extenuating circumstances made no difference.

Child abuse... I understand that sometimes it can be learnt behaviour, but it is still wrong. (Interview 32: Female, Pre-Family, Suburban Town)

Things like child abuse is always wrong whatever and there is no excuse for that. Murder is wrong but there are situations where perhaps you could understand like where a woman is constantly abused and she just flips. (Interview 61: Female, Late Family/Empty Nester, Urban City)

The only other absolute wrong named was racism.

The racists... that will always be wrong for me because that is discriminating and judgemental. (Interview 27: Female, Early/ Late Family, Urban City)

Absolute 'rights' were rather thinner on the ground, and even then voiced with great hesitation.

Things that are always right are truth, love... (Interview 56: Male, Early Family, Suburban City)

I think to save someone's life; that couldn't be wrong, could it? (Interview 29: Female, Empty Nester, Urban City)

Overall, people exercised a nuanced and intelligent attitude to morality. Moral questions were clearly important and could not be dismissed as meaningless. Absolute, unthinking relativism was very infrequent as was bland 'hang 'em and flog 'em' ethics.

Yet, there appeared to be an Achilles' heel in many moral attitudes that lay in the perceived basis for being good. As far as it was possible to tell, this lay in either reason or in emotion. Goodness was something serviceable to the individual or the social group, and not the other way round.

A handful of people recognised the weakness of both bases: reason allowed you to excuse almost anything (which some people came up against when they imaginatively and empathetically thought themselves into a victim's shoes); emotion was a predominantly subjective and enormously malleable basis for an ethical system.

Perhaps the most interesting recognition of this latter point came from one of the few respondents who claimed to see the taking of human life as an absolute wrong.

I think there is an absolute wrong. It's that you don't kill people. But what is good and what is kind is different. (Interview 39: Female, Early Family, Suburban Town)

Goodness is almost guaranteed to be confused with kindness if ethics are built on emotion.

3. Questions about the Universe

One of the most basic elements of human spirituality pertains to our understanding of and relation to creation. Exactly how we understand and relate to the universe is crucial to our self-perception as spiritual, material and psychological beings.

Questions concerning the universe featured heavily in respondents' 'one big question'. Some of these appeared relatively disinterested in nature, whilst some were clearly relevant to 'my concept of who I am'.

Respondents were asked about their understanding of the universe: whether they thought it was planned, whether it was designed, and who was 'in charge'. Stimulus material (a picture of planet earth and of a flower) was used to focus discussion. Later in the interview respondents also talked about whether they had ever felt a sense of awe and if so, what prompted it.

The results of these four areas – planning, designing, controlling, and awe – are discussed below. Broadly speaking, the consensus of opinion was that the universe was designed and awesome, but largely unplanned and uncontrolled, although there were tremendous variations of opinion within three of these four points.

3.1 Is the universe designed?

The overriding opinion was that the universe had been designed, although evidence cited in favour of this belief was varied.

The most frequently mentioned argument for design was essentially that the world worked too well for things to have come about by chance, an argument most famously articulated by William Paley at the start of the nineteenth century.

Some people think that the creation happened by chance but I think it was God who put everything in the right place. (Interview 31: Female, Student, Suburban Town)

One respondent brought a professional perspective to bear on this question.

Being in my field of expertise [as an engineer] you look at nature and you can't argue that there isn't a design for everything. The way in which it works, the shapes of leaves, the process things happen in order to make other things happen. There is a design. Obviously that has been created by something, someone. There has to be. (Interview 49: Male, Student, Suburban City)

For others it was simply inconceivable that the order around them was the result of chaos alone.

For this to evolve by chance is very remote. (Interview 3: Male, Early Family, Rural)

It is important to note that this did not necessitate the existence of God, though what it *did* imply was not always clear.

Looking at the world around us, the chances of something like this not being designed are low and inconceivable. However, I don't believe in a greater being so, and I do believe in an infinite universe so that makes everything possible. (Interview 7: Female, Student, Rural)

A handful of respondents registered a sophisticated view that combined the idea of design and evolution, in which God created the conditions for life and the universe. Once again it is worth noting that, in this instance, whilst this view does tend to point towards the existence of God, it is not necessarily the Judaeo-Christian vision of God.

All my life I have been convinced that natural laws that created those flowers so intricate and perfect there must be something pretty special behind them. I do believe in a creator but I do believe he created natural laws and everything sprung from that. He might have known that these laws would create things like that but he certainly didn't put any input or control over it after he had set it all in motion. I don't believe in any such thing as a moral God. There is no evidence for him having morals. (Interview 44: Male, Pre-Family, Suburban Town)

Given the overwhelming sense (and it was often no more than a sense) of design in the universe, respondents tended towards the view that God created the universe, although many were notably hesitant to voice this opinion (presumably for fear of sounding crass and in the awareness that they didn't have the faintest idea *how* it might have happened). Such suggestions were very often accompanied with a disarming 'they say' or 'I don't know.'

They say the universe started by the big bang, but what caused the big bang. I don't know. (Interview 24: Female, Widowed, Urban City)

Evolution [is the answer] but how it came about in the first instance, be it God, the Big Bang or universal life theory I don't know. (Interview 27: Female, Early/ Late Family, Urban City)

Not surprisingly given the complexity of the issues involved, some respondents said they simply couldn't understand the issues and, in as far as it is possible to be neutral about such issues, they were.

I am a reasonably logical person and I start to consider... and I end up with one question you see and it is an interesting one. "Who made God?" and I can't get my head around that so I stop thinking about God. (Interview 18: Male, Widowed, Rural)

There was a minority of dissenting voices, whose explanation for their lack of belief in design was that evolution disproves design, although it is worth noting that this was rarely said. Instead the word evolution was treated like some kind of magic spell that dissipated all other claims.

No, I don't think God created it all. I think evolution. (Interview 1: Female, Student, Rural)

Alternatively, the reason was that there was too much suffering in the world.

If anybody was designing this world they would make a darn site better job of it than at present in many ways (Interview 18: Male, Widowed, Rural)

The point about suffering, however, made more of a mark on respondents when they considered the *plan* rather than *design* of the universe.

3.2 Is the universe 'chance or planned'?

Attitudes to whether the universe is chance or planned were far more mixed than those concerning its design, with respondents varying from the 'totally planned' to the 'totally chance' ends of the spectrum.

The reason for this difference is interesting. The question about whether the universe is planned was understood in largely personal rather than abstract terms. The issue of the universe's design was interpreted as referring to the sense of *order* in creation, i.e. something that exists independent of human beings. In opposition to this, the issue of the universe's plan was interpreted far more anthropocentrically, i.e. as in, is *life* chance or planned? Whether the universe is chance or planned is a predominantly *human* question, the attitude to it depending far more heavily on whether things appear to be *good* rather than *ordered*.

Those at the 'all planned' end of the spectrum voiced opinions that hovered between determinism and fatalism, tending to be articulated in an 'everything has a purpose' kind of way.

There is no such thing as co-incidence. Everything happens for a reason. (Interview 49: Male, Student, Suburban City)

God gave me a date of birth and God will give me a date of death. (Interview 53: Female, Empty Nester, Suburban City)

I have always said that before you are even born it is written in a book. Everything is written and it is a life plan. Why should I worry about dying? (Interview 36: Female, Widowed, Suburban Town)

As this last quotation indicates, many of these opinions were held not on any evidential basis but for the security that such certainty affords. This could also be the case in retrospect.

I feel within my own lifetime so far there are a lot of things that have been pre-destined and I have had to overcome trials, struggles and tribulations, some quite [in]surmountable along my path but it has made me who I am today. Yes I do [believe life is planned]. (Interview 27: Female, Early/Late Family, Urban City)

It is worth noting that such opinions, while being more common among older respondents, were not restricted to them, with a number of younger respondents expressing a sense of determinism too.

At the other end of the spectrum there was the 'nothing is planned' opinion. This view had two major explanations. The first was that it was the only one compatible with the incontrovertible fact of human free will.

As soon as conscious choice is available then events cease to be pre-determined. (Interview 34: Male, Late Family, Suburban Town)

I think you make your own destiny. I seriously believe that. Nothing is planned. (Interview 29: Female, Empty Nester, Urban City)

You can't plan meeting your future partner or anything like that; that is by chance. There may be a big jigsaw up there and it has all been planned but I don't think it is... I think you are in charge of your own destiny. (Interview 23: Male, Empty Nester, Urban City)

The second was the problem of suffering. There was simply too much in the world for the universe to have beenplanned, let alone by a benevolent god. Note, incidentally, how in the second quotation here 'planned' is explicitly interpreted as 'planned for us'.

I think [it] can't be planned because why would so many horrendous things happen. (Interview 9: Female, Early Family, Rural)

I do find it a little bit difficult to think that it is planned for us all. I don't think there can be a plan to have a child murdered or anything like that. I don't actually think there is a plan. We have a choice. (Interview 45: Female, Early Family, Suburban Town)

Between these apparently diametrically opposed viewpoints a few brave respondents picked a lonely path, suggesting that the universe was guided rather than dictated, although, as with the design question, this one did not necessitate any recognisable god. Guidance could come through our free recognition that there are inherent structures and inherent values within creation, such as love.

We each have free will to do what we want but the actual fact is that we will all come to the same conclusion and that love is the only thing that works. Some learn quicker than others. (Interview 8: Female, Pre-Family, Rural)

Alternatively, it could arise when choice and fate coincide together in some (wheel-of-fortune) kind of way.

I believe that your life is very much guided by the choices and decisions you make as you go along but I also think that... opportunities are presented to you if you like, so in some way I believe in fate and co-incidence. I don't think it is a driving force but if you miss an opportunity at some stage I think things work around so that you get that opportunity again. Kind of like a wheel. (Interview 45: Female, Early Family, Suburban Town)

3.3 Who or what is in charge?

The question of planning is directly linked to that of control. Who, or what, if anyone or anything, is in charge?

A number of respondents interpreted this question as about personal control and exhibited a 'proactive' approach that made an interesting contrast to the victim mentality that is supposed to be pervasive across society today. Such responses were the natural parallel to the 'the universe is not planned' response.

I would like to think when I am a bit better that I am in control because you want to make something of your life and be happy and make other people happy. I would like to be in control. (Interview 20: Female, Pre-Family, Urban City)

If you are not happy you need to do something to change it. (Interview 45: Female, Early Family, Suburban Town)

Those respondents who answered the question with a focus on overall control of creation (rather than my control of my life) had perceptible reluctance to see God as 'in charge'. The closest that any respondent came to this view was marked by an obvious hesitation.

Obviously God, but what is God? (Interview 17: Female, Empty Nester, Rural)

Of those respondents who thought there was someone or thing in charge, an impersonal force such as 'destiny' or 'fate' was a more popular answer.

Your destiny is there and it just sort of happens. (Interview 16: Male, Late Family, Rural)

These forces could, however, be labelled as God in such a way as to sound more appealing.

I do believe that there is a reason for everything. You can't always see it at the time, but maybe in the future all will be revealed... I would have to say that God is in charge. (Interview 52: Female, Late Family, Suburban City)

A more popular view was that we are not so much controlled as guided, although this was most often expressed in personal terms.

I think we have a huge amount of control over it to a degree because we are our own people and we can steer our course, but ultimately I am sure probably we are steered in the right direction. (Interview 32: Female, Pre-Family, Suburban Town)

For others there was a kind of division of labour, so that human autonomy could combine with natural meaning in the universe.

I suppose there must be some driving force that is creating these fantastic things. I think we evolve to a certain point but I would like to think that there was somebody making things beautiful. (Interview 9: Female, Early Family, Rural)

The most popular way of describing this 'guidance' was in the familiar terms of 'watching over' me, once again underlining how anthropocentrically these questions of planning and control were interpreted.

Often I think there is someone watching over me, so I think you come back as a spirit and you do watch over your kids. (Interview 39: Female, Early Family, Suburban Town)

I think there is somebody up there watching over you, saying actually that is not the right thing to do and that is why you didn't get the job. (Interview 39: Female, Early Family, Suburban Town)

The only beliefs that might make sense to me is that within all this there is someone overseeing us in, if you like, the universe that we understand. (Interview 4: Male, Late Family, Rural)

As will be evident, this belief easily shaded over into the idea that it was spirits or relatives who were watching over me, rather than a god or creator, and even those respondents who avoided this implication were clear that just because there was (or may be) some overall guiding spirit, that didn't mean it was God. It is worth noticing how, in the following quotation, God is an 'it' rather than a 'he', how the deliberately vague word 'entities' is used and how the whole issue is in fact decided by whether good or bad things happen to people.

I have thought about that one a lot and would say if there is [a God in charge] then it is not necessarily on our side because it has allowed a very lot of bad things to happen to us and a lot of very good things. I don't really believe in the concept of a God as such that is watching over us and nudging us in the right direction. I think there are entities, I suppose, that are looking after us for whatever reason. Whether they are the entities that actually set our lives in motion in the first place I don't know. I don't believe in an ultimate God as such. I would treat that as a metaphor. (Interview 38: Male, Pre-Family, Suburban Town)

It is worth noting, too, that these views of guidance, watching over and control were not the domain of older respondents solely. Indeed, if anything, they were more frequently voiced by younger ones, such as students and pre-family respondents.

There is an interesting parallel in these responses with various quantitative surveys of recent years, which show that as scepticism towards religion and traditional religious claims has grown, so has belief in supernatural and paranormal phenomena. In 1950, 10% of people told Gallup they believed in ghosts and 2% claimed they had seen one. 48 years later MORI found that 40% of people said they believed in ghosts, 15% said they had had a personal experience of them and (alarmingly) 6% said they had based a decision on their belief in ghosts. Similarly, in 1951 7% of people said they believed in foretelling the future by cards and 6% by stars, whereas in

1998 18% of the public said they believed in fortune telling or tarot and 38% in astrology.[1]

The precise nature of these supernatural beliefs will be explored in greater detail below, but it should be noted at this stage that the British people are certainly not getting more 'rational' as religious affiliation declines and indeed may be demonstrably more superstitious and 'irrational' (a fact which some commentators have taken up cudgels against[2]). Such long-term trends do tend to suggest that religious belief has a natural role in ordering and structuring instinctive human superstition.

It is also worth pointing out, in passing, that two respondents saw control of the universe as an on-going battle within a spiritual realm, although quite how that related to the here and now was unclear.

I do believe there is a spiritual dimension beyond the physical world that we understand and there are probably forces there, some for us and some against us. The ones against us are not necessarily evil. (Interview 38: Male, Pre-Family, Suburban Town)

I think the devil comes into his own sometimes. I think the Lord has a lot to do with a lot of things but I do think we have got to fight the devil. (Interview 30: Female, Separated, Urban City)

---

1   MORI, *British Public Opinion Newsletter*(Vol. XXVI, No. 1, Summer 2003)

2   See, for example, Francis Wheen, *How mumbo-jumbo conquered the world: A short history of modern delusions*(Fourth Estate, 2004)

3.4 A sense of awe?

Of the four distinct 'universe' questions – design, planning, control and awe – only the last received a clear and unambiguous response. Did creation afford respondents a sense of awe? The overwhelming answer was 'Yes' with the sheer range of examples cited being particularly interesting.

These included the usual experiences of sunsets, landscapes, eclipses, and birth, but there was also a wide range of other, less obvious sources, including the birth of an animal:

I've seen a calf being born. It wasn't breathing. It was so tiny. So I did all the things you do. Like lift them up, shake them and get all the mucus out and she came to life and started breathing. It was so brilliant. That gave me a sense of awe. Her eyes had gone all cloudy like they do and then she started spluttering and it was brilliant. (Interview 1: Female, Student, Rural)

Going clubbing:

Walking into a nightclub with the mass of people, the music and dancing, laughter and happiness. That is awe-inspiring. (Interview 7: Female, Student, Rural)

A funeral:

The funeral I was at was being taken care of by God. I wouldn't say anything supernatural about it, but I did believe he was taking everybody's pain on board. (Interview 26: Male, Pre-Family, Urban City)

Mathematics:

A multitude of places from a small wayside flower on a walk to the slightly higher intellectual realisation that the math-

ematical construction of that tiny little thing has got so many resonances throughout the creation of the human body and grass and trees. There is a mathematical formula for everything that exists. (Interview 10: Male, Late Family, Rural)

And material possessions:

Jumping into a new vehicle worth a lot of money. Meeting somebody very famous. (Interview 3: Male, Early Family, Rural)

Other experiences mentioned included Sydney Harbour and Bridge, the Louvre, National Gallery, being at sea, castles, acting, flying in a helicopter, World War I Battlefields, cemeteries, and megaliths.

The ubiquity, range and strength of awe as a reaction to the world is very interesting. Even the most jaded, cynical or 'rational' respondents claimed to experience it. There was no division by age, life-stage or sex, although inevitably those who had experienced the birth of their children often mentioned that as one of the most awe-inspiring experiences of their life. To be human, it seems, is to be awed.

The universe, then, was seen as awesome, ordered, almost certainly designed, perhaps guided, maybe planned but probably not controlled. People's understanding was self-confessedly insufficient, profoundly anthropocentric and often hesitant. Creation, in particular its design, clearly pointed towards a designer, although often in a rather simplistic way. Then again, in its apparent disorder *from a human point of view* it pointed away from God. Whichever stance one took, it still took one's breath away and at least encouraged metaphysical contemplation, even if it didn't bring one to the point of believing in God.

4. Questions about God

What effect do people's beliefs – their attitude to the universe, to their own destiny, to life's purpose or lack of it – have on their non/belief and attitude to God and to the existence of a 'spiritual' realm? The following two sections examine these questions, although do not touch on people's attitude to and understanding of distinctive Christian issues, such as Jesus, the Bible, heaven and hell, which are dealt with in section B below.

4.1 Do you believe in God?

Before examining respondents' belief in and attitudes to God it is important to remember that respondents were recruited as non-churchgoers. As quantitative research over recent years has shown, there is little correlation between belief in God and attendance at a religious service. According to the British Social Attitudes survey (1998) around 70% of people are theists of some kind and a further 15% agnostic, with only 10% of people saying they didn't believe in God. According to research conducted by ICM for the BBC's programme 'What the world thinks of God', 46% of Britons said they had always believed in God, 10% that they hadn't used to but do now, and 11% that they believed in a higher power rather than God. This compared to 16% who declared themselves agnostic and 12% who claimed not to believe in God but who did consider themselves to be spiritual people.

At the same time, best estimates suggest that around one in eight of the population attends a weekly religious service and fewer still a weekly Christian service. The result, as far as our sample was concerned, was that although their responses reflect a wide spectrum of a/theistic beliefs in the UK, they do not reflect the *whole* spectrum, with orthodox Christian (and other) believers being excluded Having recognised this, it will become clear that one of the striking features of the responses was how much belief there was from people who had very little or no inclination to attend a religious service.

A small minority of respondents entirely dismissed the idea of God as something made up, usually for reasons of self-assurance. Such responses were often based on the idea that God was a primitive scientific theory.

A supernatural entity which people created, to cover all the answers to the questions they didn't know. (Interview 1: Female, Student, Rural)

Even that explanation didn't necessarily mean there wasn't a 'God' of some kind for some, however.

I believe that God is what man has created in order to make sense of himself. That is not to say that God doesn't exist or that there is not a power. (Interview 35: Female, Empty Nester, Suburban Town)

A slightly greater proportion was hesitant but more inclined to disbelieve than to believe. The God they disbelieved in was sometimes something of a caricature.

The problem about it is that I can't relate to a man with a big beard sitting on a cloud somewhere. That does not feel real to me. (Interview 32: Female, Pre-Family, Suburban Town)

Alternatively, God was incredible because 'religion causes so many wars' (an interesting example of how one completely unrelated, not to mention questionable, fact can be used to disprove another.)

I like to think that humanity is growing out of the need for a personal god... there is so much going on in the world which I find disturbing because it so much relates to the assumption that there is a personal god. Blowing themselves up to be martyrs, for example. (Interview 34: Male, Late Family, Suburban Town)

Another respondent gave a similar but slightly more credible and certainly more heartfelt reason for this disbelief. She came from one of the poorest backgrounds of all the interviewees.

I am not saying that there isn't a god, but my understanding is that he is supposed to be this great man who saved the world, started the world and sent Jesus to help us all, but Jesus has not yet knocked my door. He ain't helped me one iota.... God sent him [Jesus] but he never sent him to me. (Interview 21: Female, Early Family, Urban City)

Equally heartfelt, though not so much based on personal circumstances, was one respondent's inability to believe in spite of her desire to do so. Such belief required a clear and incontrovertible sign.

I would love to believe. That is my whole thing; I would love to believe but however hard I try or don't try; I have never had any kind of sign to me personally. (Interview 17: Female, Empty Nester, Rural)

More common still was a certain vagueness and uncertainty. Some respondents said they didn't know whether they believed or not and others sat on the fence because they did not have the proof they wanted.

Is there a god...? I sit on the fence and have done so from the age of about ten. I don't know where I stand. I think if I knew for definite... It is not blind faith, but you just trust. I don't have that because I don't really know. (Interview 32: Female, Pre-Family, Suburban Town)

The most common single position was one of hesitant and vague belief.

I do believe God is of a higher power. From time to time I had faith in him and lost faith in him. I have prayed and when things didn't go well at all I lost faith because I thought my prayers weren't being answered. (Interview 26: Male, Pre-Family, Urban City)

Well, I suppose you could go to science and dismiss God altogether but I think there is some sort of supreme power that is shaping our world, but what I don't know. (Interview 17: Female, Empty Nester, Rural)

Finally there was a small minority of respondents who dismissed atheism altogether, expressing a certainty one would more naturally expect to hear from a single-minded believer.

I think people who say they are an atheist have not thought about it. It is a massive statement to make. I think these days people find it difficult to relate to most religions, not just Christianity, unless they are trendy at the time, like Buddhism or whatever is coming out at the time. (Interview 32: Female, Pre-Family, Suburban Town)

I think there are people who are not spiritually or not intellectually very mature. Some people can't benefit from having therapy, in the same way that some people can't be spiritually minded enough to grasp things that are highly academic in some ways. (Interview 35: Female, Empty Nester, Suburban Town)

4.2 What is God like?

Given the vagueness of belief in God, perceptions of his/its characteristics and nature were unclear. A number of people spoke of the stereotype, although most were quick to dismiss it.

I always imagine him sitting on a chair in a white robe and just watching. (Interview 6: Female, Widowed, Rural)

If I was to go back to the church which I was brought up through I would picture God in white behind the pearly gates with Jesus by his side and angels with wings and stuff. My own sense tells me that it is not a literal thing, God. It is every positive part of energy within the universe. (Interview 56: Male, Early Family, Suburban City)

The issue of Old versus New Testament portrayals was brought up by one respondent.

I understand there to be two basic concepts of God which are revealed through the Bible. The Old Testament God being the creator, wrath, torturing people like the book of Job and then you have the New Testament version of painting God as a father or shepherd looking after his flock... I see all of those beliefs as being metaphors. (Interview 38: Male, Pre-Family, Suburban Town)

More bluntly one respondent remarked of the biblical view of God:

There are a lot of people out there [who] feel that the descriptions that the Church or Bible give would insult their intelligence. (Interview 56: Male, Early Family, Suburban City)

Instead God's characteristics were predominantly abstract. Words like energy, spirit and love were popular.

I would imagine him to be energy. (Interview 44: Male, Pre-Family, Suburban Town)

A spirit that overlooks everybody. I think that it is somebody who, if you wish to, is somebody you can turn to. (Interview 2: Male, Pre-Family, Rural)

A spiritual force; an energy that runs and flows between all of us. God is within us, the spiritual force is within us. I tend to call the force the great spirit. (Interview 58: Female, Late Family, Suburban City)

I class God as another word for Love. (Interview 48: Female, Widowed, Suburban Town)

I think it is a manifestation of all things good. I say 'It' rather than He or She. In many respects that is where I start sailing close to the wind because I don't see a God as sitting on a cloud struggling with a harp and all that. I see it in a much more tangible theory/concept, intellectually as well as religiously. (Interview 10: Male, Late Family, Rural)

The idea that he/it somehow had an overseeing role regarding creation, an idea that did not necessarily sit easily with people's opinions regarding the planning of the universe, was also popular.

A being or thing that is all-seeing, all-knowing, all-intelligent or spiritual that we worship or who we have to answer to when we die. (Interview 26: Male, Pre-Family, Urban City)

An all omnipresent, all-powerful spirit that controls things. (Interview 51: Female, Early Family, Suburban City)

70

Phenomenon who oversees and through his son is able to influence and understand the totality of where we are. (Interview 4: Male, Late Family, Rural)

It was easier for some to see God as an intellectual concept rather than a personal being, although this could leave a tension.

All knowing, loving, caring. [I] can't call God a person, but I think of him as a person. (Interview 3: Male, Early Family, Rural)

These opinions of God's nature were brought out clearly in people's answers to the question where God was. Locating him in space or time was usually considered ridiculous and responses tended toward the mystical. God was everywhere.

I would say everywhere. He is a free roaming spirit. (Interview 2: Male, Pre-Family, Rural)

Everywhere. God the creator and God the universe and I would go with God the universe, he is everywhere and in everything. (Interview 38: Male, Pre-Family, Suburban Town)

Everywhere you find peace, God is. I suppose he is in war torn places as well. (Interview 36: Female, Widowed, Suburban Town)

Or he was within me.

God is within me as well as without. Love is in my heart and that is God. It is within and about. God is within everything. (Interview 8: Female, Pre-Family, Rural)

Right in here, deep inside. I don't know how to describe it really. When you talk to this higher being it is away from

*yourself but very close. (Interview 61: Female, Late Family/
Empty Nester, Urban City)*

Or he was in a different dimension.

*I read something years and years ago... it was called the 'flat
earth' theory. What you have to imagine is that the world is
actually flat and only exists in two dimensions so you have all
these flat people and everything is flat but there is a third
dimension which we know about but the flat earthies won't be
able to understand it because they only know about two
dimensions. Therefore if there is a fourth dimension that we
don't know about, maybe that is where God is, I don't know.
(Interview 18: Male, Widowed, Rural)*

Generally speaking, ideas were plentiful but haphazard, with a
tension running through interviewees (or, more precisely, the
majority who could at least countenance the existence of God)
between the abstract, transcendent God who was credible and
intellectually defensible and the personal, immanent one who
was neither of these things but was, on the other hand, rather
more interesting and relevant to me.

4.3 What is the relationship between God and human beings?

This tension between transcendence and immanence naturally
impacted people's opinion of God and man's relationship.

At one end of the spectrum was the view that God could not
possibly be interested in humans. He (it) would simply be too
big and complex to be bothered with us.

*If there is some sort of, I don't like to use the word
supernatural, some sort of being on whom the existence of the
universe depends then that being, by definition, would have to*

be so vast and complex that even beginning to understand would be far beyond any human given the scale and perplexity of the universe. I find it extremely difficult to believe in such an entity that would have such a detailed interest in individual beings as insignificant as we are. (Interview 34: Male, Late Family, Suburban Town)

The same respondent did, however, register the possibility of there being a relationship of sorts, although it was not one to which he was willing to acquiesce.

Far too many people understand the word God as an ancient white-bearded control freak on a cloud up in the sky somewhere... I wouldn't be surprised if the laws of the universe didn't accommodate some higher order of entity which gets its kicks out of watching the way we muck around and wishes to be worshipped but on the other hand if such an entity does exist I don't think we should be indulging it. (Interview 34: Male, Late Family, Suburban Town)

This question of why or how God might be interested in people did not interest many other respondents, however. This was not because they had better ideas than this interviewee but because they seemed to think it came with the territory. If God existed 'he' would be interested, almost by definition, in human beings.

There was no real reason for this. God's interest in mankind was treated almost as an axiom, possibly because, as some respondents implied, mankind was, almost by definition, interested in God. The human interest in God was often put down to need, a fact that, when cited, was often used to dismiss God's existence. For some, man's need of God precludes God existence.

I think they have to relate to God. They are terrified of the fact that he might not be there. (Interview 44: Male, Pre-Family, Suburban Town)

For some, this arrangement was in fact healthy, despite being untrue; something like a noble lie.

I don't think there is a God up there but I think that all good believers have got God in their mind and think of him as an old man with a beard and when they are in trouble they think about him and when they go out for a walk they try to get inspiration from him. God can't do anything for you but he can help you do something for yourself... Let's keep the thought of him alive. Don't ever think, say or even think anything about people that think they rely on the presence of God – that is their prerogative. That is their prop. (Interview 11: Male, Empty Nester, Rural)

I don't think science will ever find it. I hope nobody ever works out a theory to prove that God doesn't exist. (Interview 26: Male, Pre-Family, Urban City)

If the human side of the relationship was marked by dependence, God's side provided guidance, comfort and possibly judgement.

I believe there is a greater being and I think you are judged the whole time you are living. (Interview 13: Female, Student, Rural)

He gives guidance to the people on the earth and the world would be very peaceful if everyone followed him. There would be no war, no hunger, no hatred. (Interview 33: Male, Early Family, Suburban Town)

One of God's primary roles was simply to be there.

Someone you call upon if you are in distress or when you haven't got anyone else to talk to. (Interview 29: Female, Empty Nester, Urban City)

Although prayer was treated as a separate topic within the interviews, it did, perhaps inevitably, come up as an aspect of the discussion about this God-human relationship. Mankind could, at least according to some respondents, communicate with God in such a way that offered comfort *–whether or not God was there.*

There are times when you are sitting there praying, it doesn't really matter whether there is or isn't because it is still comforting, to have that feeling. (Interview 37: Male, Student, Suburban Town)

You are not going to get any answers from it but you are going to get all your worries off your back, which should help to sort of relieve the stress. (Interview 2: Male, Pre-Family, Rural)

I just feel comfortable and usually to be honest whenever I have done that, prayed for something. (Interview 45: Female, Early Family, Suburban Town)

You feel that you have done something and it makes you feel better in yourself. (Interview 16: Male, Late Family, Rural)

It also offered you guidance.

It puts you on the right track. (Interview 15: Female, Early Family, Rural)

Providing you are willing to accept his answer and it might not necessarily be the one you want then, yes, there is a communication there. (Interview 52: Female, Late Family, Suburban City)

Thus, irrespective of its actual efficacy, communicating with God actually made a difference.

It makes a difference to me because I think I am doing something positive. Sometimes it works but sometimes it doesn't but if it doesn't well, hey, it was just not meant to be. (Interview 39: Female, Early Family, Suburban Town)

Once again, this attitude was to be found across ages, from the young women above to the older one below. It was a notably more female response, however. It is interesting to notice, incidentally, the treatment of the word 'religious' in this following quotation. The respondent, not among the more hostile of interviewees, was determined not to be labelled religious, in spite of her beliefs and actions.

[Interviewer: You definitely believe that there is a god?] Yes, absolutely. [Do you think you can communicate with this god?] Yes, I think it is necessary to pray. I wouldn't describe myself as a religious person but I certainly believe in God and I certainly believe in the power of prayer. (Interview 54: Female, Widowed, Suburban City)

Similarly, another elderly respondent defiantly distanced herself from the word 'pray' although she admitted talking to God 'most of the time'. Talking to God (however intimately) was, it seemed, a slightly different phenomenon to prayer, less 'religious' and hence more credible.

If I have got problems I go to the big man upstairs… I talk to him. I don't pray, I just talk. I talk to him most of the time… I usually say good morning to him and goodnight to him when I go to bed; he is just there. I sometimes worry I take him for granted. I said to him this morning "You know sometimes Lord, I must disappoint you very much and I know I am not supposed to take you for granted." (Interview 36: Female, Widowed, Suburban Town)

There was also a sizeable minority of respondents who were rather less impressed by the lack of an answer from prayer, and quite unwilling to smile on the activity for its positive psychological benefits. A one-way conversation was not enough.

He doesn't really talk back does he? You are speaking to yourself most of the time. (Interview 20: Female, Pre-Family, Urban City)

There is nothing and there has never been anything that makes me feel that I am having a two way conversation, you know? I've always given it respect, but it has never felt real to me. (Interview 32: Female, Pre-Family, Suburban Town)

One or two respondents were also irate at the idea of praying to God in a supplicatory fashion. If we are to have a relationship with God, it should be a relationship between equals.

I mean, if he loves us all as his own children and wants us to follow in his footsteps and be good, why does he expect us to bow down on our knees to ask him for something? (Interview 21: Female, Early Family, Urban City)

The most common form of communication mentioned was when respondents described talking with God, on their own terms, according to their own needs, and with a detachment that indemnified them against the charge that prayer was infantile or futile. The God these respondents spoke about was not the intellectual concept that might exist but the personal being who probably didn't but was useful nonetheless. This kind of communication veered towards the contemplative.

77

I choose a place outside alone just to sit and think... I can say there have been a few times when I have felt that I have been connected to something bigger than myself. It happened just for a split second but it did happen and I just felt as if I had jumped up higher and could see everything for a split second and then come straight back down and then it is forgotten. I can't explain it at all. Whether that was the touch of God in some form, I don't know. (Interview 38: Male, Pre-Family, Suburban Town)

Sometimes I do just talk and hope that there is somebody at the other end. If I know there is something bad happening I just pray that we will get over it. (Interview 20: Female, Pre-Family, Urban City)

If you are anything like me you only do [it] when you want something and that is terrible. We have all done it, you know "if this happens God I will never do that again". I think that is a very human thing and you shouldn't do that. (Interview 45: Female, Early Family, Suburban Town)

For such a relationship, actual communication was not necessary. Being still was sufficient.

How I relate to the great being ... is by being still. (Interview 58: Female, Late Family, Suburban City)

Crucially important was the idea that the relationship's communication could take place anywhere.

I don't think there is any specific place where you are meant to communicate with him. (Interview 19: Male, Student, Urban City)

You can talk, pray, anytime, all the time, wherever, it doesn't matter. (Interview 52: Female, Late Family, Suburban City)

It emphatically did not need to be in a church.

You can go to church and worship but I believe anybody can pray to God and that is why I don't necessarily go to church every week. (Interview 13: Female, Student, Rural)

I don't think you have to go to church to relate to him. If you believe in him he is always there for you and overlooking you. (Interview 20: Female, Pre-Family, Urban City)

It could quite easily be in your bedroom, unseen, with the door closed.

I used to go quite often but ... if I really feel that I need guidance or want to say a prayer, I will quite often do it upstairs in my bedroom. (Interview 15: Female, Early Family, Rural)

Finally, one respondent observed that our potential relationship with God is shaped by our own relational health and abilities in just the same way as all our other relationships are.

I think we are all relating in our own unique way to our own unique understanding of what God, the Father, or a father, or my father... We can only relate to God within our own experience of relating to other people and things. Some people don't know how to relate. They don't have very good relationship abilities... So if you have a relationship problem in you for whatever reason, then it is going to limit your ability to relate to your own family let alone a heavenly father. (Interview 35: Female, Empty Nester, Suburban Town)

God was, therefore, a curiously divided character. Outside the very small minority who dismissed 'him' altogether, God assumed two distinct forms. On the one hand there was the interesting and perhaps credible theory, an abstract explanation for all there is (whether that is the universe's design, its very existence or the laws of nature) who was believable but somewhat remote and frankly irrelevant to my life. On the other, there was a personal God, not necessarily an intimate 'he', still less the loving father of the Bible, but certainly more immediate and personal than the abstract, theoretical God.

Respondents were, by and large, somewhat reluctant to admit to believing in this God for fear of appearing childish or naïve. The personal God was altogether less credible than the abstract theory. Yet, many did still pray or communicate with 'him' in some way, driven, it appeared, by some innate need that overrode the apparent absurdity of the activity. Thus respondents protected themselves from potential accusations of wish-fulfilment by willingly recognising the possibility of God's non-existence whilst at the same time lauding the positive effect of that relationship. In those cases, the relationship occurred *in spite* of what people believed rather than because of it.

The tension in all this was noted and the frustration with 'one-way' conversations or the inefficacy of prayer was often remarked on. Yet for a God whose existence was questionable, nature largely unfamiliar and whereabouts completely unknown, there was a surprising amount of relating going on.

5. Questions about the Spiritual Realm

As already mentioned, quantitative research has shown that people in the UK today are decidedly 'spiritual' (or, at least, inclined to claim they are spiritual). Asking people directly what they think about 'spiritual reality' is not easy, however, with both the words 'spiritual' and 'reality' being open to a myriad of interpretations.

For this reason, respondents were given a list of phenomena and asked to react to each. These included magic, prayer, meditation, angels, ghosts, trances, miracles, aliens, déjà vu, horoscopes, premonitions, and out of body experiences.

For reasons of time, not every respondent reacted to every concept in detail and so it is not feasible to offer a robust idea of the proportion of people who believe in a 'spiritual reality' (not that qualitative research should be used to calculate such proportions anyway).

The overall picture however, was of two kinds of spiritual experience. The first was inherently less credible or meaningful and was often dismissed unless the individual themselves, or a close and reliable friend, had experienced it personally. Trances, premonitions, visions, out-of-body experiences, and, perhaps strangely, horoscopes fell into this category. The second group was disparate, including ghosts, miracles, angels, and prayer. Respondents tended to be more interested and engaged in these phenomena and were less willing to dismiss them. They were inherently more credible although this did not necessarily mean they were more likely to have had an impact on an individual's life, even when that individual purported to have experienced it.

5.1 Areas generally dismissed

Of those ideas that were most readily dismissed, **magic** was paramount. It was a con, a thing of children's parties, a trick.

There is no such thing as magic. Magic is a man made thing. (Interview 49: Male, Student, Suburban City)

[Magic is] entertainment and something to be disbelieved. (Interview 11: Male, Empty Nester, Rural)

Magic is conjuring and something very much for children. (Interview 12: Male, Widowed, Rural)

Only one respondent interpreted it in a more positive way but this was clearly down to a more figurative use of the word.

Magic for me is a wonderful experience. Things that have happened to me and my children's lives, like birth, creation, seeing things grow. (Interview 52: Female, Late Family, Suburban City)

Trances, too, were readily dismissed as spiritual experiences, although largely because it was an unfamiliar term to most respondents, except possibly for those who connected it to drugs.

It was hallucinogenically induced... It was transcendental, felt good. I felt it was very spiritual and in touch with things but was cheating really... I think it is a little more fun if you get there yourself. It would be fun without using these substances. (Interview 44: Male, Pre-Family, Suburban Town)

There are so many ways to take that one [i.e. trances]. Self-induced state through meditation, contemplation or maybe drug induced or hypnotism. Whole can of worms that one. (Interview 10: Male, Late Family, Rural)

Déjà vu was slightly more commonly experienced but carried with it little or no spiritual meaning.

I do very much so always get, if you like, déjà vu. (Interview 49: Male, Student, Suburban City)

I've had things happen where I think I've had things like this happen before. (Interview 48: Female, Widowed, Suburban Town)

Horoscopes were commonly dismissed, both as spiritually meaningful and indeed as meaningful in any way, although there were some exceptions.

That is something that does make me think. You know the movement of the stars and the pattern, you know like the North Star. They could have an impact on my daily life. (Interview 37: Male, Student, Suburban Town)

Astrology is a very precise art and very valuable. (Interview 8: Female, Pre-Family, Rural)

This general dismissal of horoscopes is not easy to square with their widespread use in society, and may be a result of respondents not wishing to appear credulous and, at the same time, genuinely not taking horoscopes seriously, reading them primarily for entertainment.

Premonitions and **visions** received slightly more credence although again they did not seem to have any real significance, spiritual or otherwise.

I often have dreams and not long after something will happen and I remember dreaming about it. (Interview 20: Female, Pre-Family, Urban City)

I went to see Gypsy Rose Lee in Great Yarmouth and everything she told me has come true. It is so scary, but that is the only lady who has ever told me something that has come so true to the point, where other people you see just rip you off. (Interview 15: Female, Early Family, Rural)

I believe in visions and when my children were little, they used to come to me and say that they had seen things. Certainly my eldest daughter saw grandma and she had never seen a picture of her or knew what she looked like or anything. This lady appeared at the top of the stairs and that was her. (Interview 58: Female, Late Family, Suburban City)

One respondent tried to explain the phenomenon.

There are people out there who are susceptible to this wavelength. Their minds are a little bit freer or maybe through practice they open up a bit more. (Interview 56: Male, Early Family, Suburban City)

A few more were openly sceptical about it.

I am never entirely sure whether premonitions are not self-fulfilling prophecy. (Interview 34: Male, Late Family, Suburban Town)

Just a game. There are logical extrapolations of evidence and therefore you could argue it is a simple scientific thing. It is a bit of a guessology. (Interview 10: Male, Late Family, Rural)

Generally speaking, premonitions and visions were treated as strange but credible aspects of the world.

There was a similar attitude to **out-of-body experiences**, although one that was entirely limited to personal experience. Those who had experienced them (or had reliable friends who had) were open and involved with the phenomenon. Those who had not, dismissed it or were simply not interested.

I haven't [experienced one] but I know a good friend who has... that was when he had a very bad accident, so he was being revived at the time... My understanding of that is when you leave your body as such and become soul-like so you are looking down on yourself and the situation you are in. (Interview 32: Female, Pre-Family, Suburban Town)

I have had two but they were when I was in my 20s. Involuntary ones and they frightened me to death because I didn't know what was happening. I felt myself spinning around the bedroom, looking at myself on the bed, miraculously not hitting the walls, but if I had I now know that I wouldn't have hurt myself because I wasn't in the body. The other one was flying up the road, I can only say flying because that was the experience, Albany Road, Stockingford where I used to live and cars all under me and I was frightened to death. (Interview 58: Female, Late Family, Suburban City)

5.2 Areas of interest and openness

Aliens were commonly thought to exist, although opinion was divided about whether they actually had contacted or visited earth in any way. The main reasons for people's positive attitude towards them were the size of the universe and the perceived arrogance in asserting our uniqueness or solitude.

I definitely can't see that we would be the only ones when you see the size of the universe. (Interview 49: Male, Student, Suburban City)

I think it is quite arrogant to believe that we are the only living force within the universe. (Interview 32: Female, Pre-Family, Suburban Town)

No... there may be life on distant planets as it is a huge galaxy far bigger than we can imagine, so it would be silly to think that there was not something going on somewhere else but I don't believe in parallel universe or anything like that. (Interview 51: Female, Early Family, Suburban City)

One respondent claimed to have had an actual encounter with an alien.

When I first went to Tysoe I was lying in bed quite early in the morning and there was this thing next to me, which was quite frightening. I was lying on my front and there was this quite leathery creature a bit like a flat tortoise with fingers that had no flesh, just bony fingers. It was a chocolatey colour and I was really frightened and it went away. Then I was sad because I realised it only wanted to be friendly. I was put off by its appearance. After that a couple of times I went out to the loo and there were these bright areas and I thought they were harvest vehicles working at night or farms. It wasn't that sort of light though, it was a hazy light. Four of them. And I told Grace and she said yes, other people had had sightings of UFOs there. I then wondered if this brown creature had come from there but it didn't tell me anything. (Interview 8: Female, Pre-Family, Rural)

Only one respondent dismissed the possibility of aliens entirely, describing it as *'more bunkum. Total and utter rubbish.' (Interview 18: Male, Widowed, Rural)*

Needless to say aliens, as conceived and discussed, had no spiritual import for respondents. In the same way, the idea of

communicating with another world was interpreted, in the main, in a physical, scientific way.

To communicate with another world is definitely possible and I believe they are communicating and there are people around us who are not from this world, but we can't see it because we are not that highly evolved as a society on the whole. (Interview 49: Male, Student, Suburban City)

Some respondents put a spiritual interpretation on the phrase and responded to it positively. For them 'plane' or 'dimension' were preferable terms, as they avoided any confusion.

Maybe a different plane but not world. Yes I do. There was a time in my life where I practised as a medium. To tell somebody and to be so descriptive about someone's life... you cannot pick time after time information... that is so personal. To have the person sat opposite you and to be verified and to be accurate, yes I do [think it is possible]. (Interview 27: Female, Early/ Late Family, Urban City)

One respondent tried to explain the phenomenon of communicating with another 'plane'.

Yes I do. We only use a small part of our brain anyway and some people can be tuned in. (Interview 17: Female, Empty Nester, Rural)

The idea of such spiritual communication was also dismissed, however, with one respondent remarking, *'I think you can make yourself believe that you are.' (Interview 2: Male, Pre-Family, Rural)*

A handful of respondents added examples of similar phenomena to the list they were being asked to consider. One claimed that we had **psychic powers**.

I feel that we have all got latent psychic power within us and if necessary if God wanted to develop that, one could. (Interview 58: Female, Late Family, Suburban City)

Another felt that some people had **healing powers**.

I have been told many times by people with psychic powers or when I have had a massage done that I have a power to heal people. I find that quite odd actually. Heal people verbally in conversation. (Interview 27: Female, Early/Late Family, Urban City)

A third spoke openly about the existence of 'spirits'.

There are good and bad spirits and some earthbound spirits, trapped as they went over. (Interview 27: Female, Early/Late Family, Urban City)

Two others talked about having spiritual experiences **through 'nature'**, by which they meant not the sense of awe that most people registered but receiving specific communication, encouragement, support, or even a kind of emotional healing through the unusual behaviour of animals. Their stories bore similarities and were both moving in their own way, the second having echoes of reincarnation.

When my dad died it was a very sad time and we used to go to the woods and it was winter and very cold, nothing around, but this one little robin came from nowhere and I think it was my brother said, "Watch that robin, it's going to come right up to us". Its behaviour wasn't normal. It was almost like it was trying to communicate with us. It did seem very memorable and we will all to this day never forget that little robin. (Interview 3: Male, Early Family, Rural)

I look at a robin in the garden and think well, 'is that you John come back to see me?' Funny things like that. I always remember when my granddad died. A stray dog turned up on our doorstep. We couldn't find out who it belonged to. We phoned the police and everything but we just kept it, but we referred to this dog as being granddad coming back again. (Interview 6: Female, Widowed, Rural)

One other respondent described a powerful spiritual experience, a kind of epiphany based on **love**.

I don't know whether it was the great presence talking to me but I did have and I have never forgotten it but I had this message. I heard this voice and the voice said to me, this was years ago, "The answer is in all creation". I have never forgotten it because it was so powerful it literally blew my head apart. There is no other way to put it. This voice said "The answer is in all creation" and it scared me to be honest at that time and I didn't know what the hell was going on. I had my beliefs before then but after that it came to me. "The answer is in all Creation" and it is Love, that is the answer, and it was fantastic. (Interview 58: Female, Late Family, Suburban City)

These responses were individual, isolated reactions which had meaning and import to the people who voiced them. In that respect they were unlike the general attitudes to magic, trances, déjà vu, horoscopes, premonitions, visions, out-of-body experiences and aliens that, if they had any spiritual connotation at all, had little spiritual significance for these respondents.

The other spiritual areas discussed – ghosts, miracles, angels, prayer and meditation – were different in that personal interest and involvement in them was far greater, although this only rarely stretched to them having a significant impact on an individual's life. It is worth noting that, with the exception of meditation, these are all more traditional spiritual areas, although the attitude to and interpretation of them was often far from traditional.

Ghosts were a topic of considerable interest. Opinions as to their existence were mixed, although probably more for than against. Those who believed in them tended to see them as souls that had yet to find rest, though there was also a propensity to describe them in pseudo-scientific terms ('energy', 'discarnate', 'entity') in order to make them seem a little more respectable.

A ghost to me is someone who has lived on this earth and has died and their soul for whatever reason is still here... has unfinished work. (Interview 32: Female, Pre-Family, Suburban Town)

I do believe and that is probably why I think there is more after we die. More than just a being or a body. (Interview 45: Female, Early Family, Suburban Town)

Energy passing into spirit. (Interview 56: Male, Early Family, Suburban City)

They are discarnate entities that are still earthbound and they haven't gone on to the place where they need to be and sometimes they need a little bit of help to go. (Interview 58: Female, Late Family, Suburban City)

Those who disbelieved in them did so either because they had not personally experienced them or because they smelt of hocus-pocus.

I have never seen one and until I do I am not going to believe in them. I think they are stories made up to frighten people. (Interview 47: Male, Empty Nester, Suburban Town)

I don't believe because I haven't seen one. I don't believe anything I haven't seen. (Interview 28: Female, Empty Nester, Urban City)

I do not in any way shape or form believe in ghosts, spiritualism, mind reading, séances, or anything like that and the main reason is because I have read and know enough to realise that an awful lot of people have been duped by these people. (Interview 18: Male, Widowed, Rural)

At least five respondents admitted to having personal experience (statistics should never be culled from qualitative research but one cannot help but remark how high this proportion is). Some were notably vague.

There was a point where I thought I was with a ghost or some sort of energy. (Interview 56: Male, Early Family, Suburban City)

We used to hear things. I did my work experience with Mary and one time we could hear these footsteps in the hall. We opened the window and there was nothing there. It was horrible. Sometimes you could feel that there was something behind you, but there wasn't. (Interview 20: Female, Pre-Family, Urban City)

Others were more precise.

I have had two experiences in the last two years. I was in the kitchen, in the toilet and the toilet door was open and a figure walked through the front door... they had no feet but the head and clothes were my mother and she walked in. When I described the clothes I was told that the black and white photograph of my mother in those clothes were what she wore for my brother's wedding and I was only eight. Don't ask me why I saw that. (Interview 53: Female, Empty Nester, Suburban City)

I saw a ghost once. I was in bed and again it was early morning. I heard this tapping and thought it was a cat and realised I don't have a cat. It was just a being there at the end of the bed and I was really frightened. It went away and came back two or three times. I was frightened each time and eventually I spoke to somebody about it and they said well it wants your help. It is a being and it is trapped in your house. This was in London. She told me to do this ritual with a candle. You ring a bell in each corner of the room and sprinkle salted water to clear it. Then she said next time it comes just tell it to go to where it is meant to be. I was so scared and could hardly get the words out of my mouth... Anyway I managed to get it out and it was wonderful because as soon as I said it I saw it rise up all happy and it just went up in a column of white light. It didn't come back. (Interview 8: Female, Pre-Family, Rural)

Still others were equally specific but unwilling to say the word.

When I was about 18 I was in a car with a lot of other people. This sounds stereotypical but we backed into a church late at night in Streatham in London. I just happened to look over to this gravestone and there was a lady standing by this grave and I remember thinking, 'Oh God, fancy standing by a grave.' I looked around and looked back and suddenly realised that it was some sort of... I don't know. (Interview 61: Female, Late Family/ Empty Nester, Urban City)

Those other spiritual beings, **angels**, cropped up even more commonly though in thoroughly personalised guises. A handful of people registered the traditional, often hackneyed image of angels, in such a way as implied their non-existence.

I suppose imaginary good things – people-ish. Flying people. (Interview 31: Female, Student, Suburban Town)

Very lovely kids with wings in a white dress and they can fly. Golden/ginger hair, lovely legs. (Interview 33: Male, Early Family, Suburban Town)

Far more common was the idea that angels were people who had died. This could be people who had been conspicuously good:

Real decent people within society who have passed away. Like Mother Teresa. (Interview 2: Male, Pre-Family, Rural)

Or (more commonly) relatives:

My grandfather. The night he died I was young and he was on the other side of the world. He came to me and said he would not be around and I do still feel in times of crisis a warm sense. (Interview 9: Female, Early Family, Rural)

Or just people generally:

I love the idea that you become an angel when you die. (Interview 50: Female, Pre-Family, Suburban City)

There are some people who have reached a state of consciousness which is a higher level than some of us.

Whether that is an angel, well maybe. (Interview 10: Male, Late Family, Rural)

I just remember in my younger life that when I lost a cousin, he was the most beautiful child. And my mother said to me, 'He's too good. He's an angel and that is why they've taken him'. (Interview 6: Female, Widowed, Rural)

Nothing was known about these deceased beings except that they had a role in watching over you, in much the same way as some respondents claimed that the person or thing ultimately in charge of the universe did.

I believe greatly in angels and that they help you. I haven't personally come across one yet. (Interview 13: Female, Student, Rural)

I don't necessarily think of people with floating wings but there are guardian angels that will look after people. (Interview 32: Female, Pre-Family, Suburban Town)

Every living thing has an angel, which is like a blueprint of you – you in your perfected form – God's thought of you. It stands behind you all the time. If you are in need you can rest your head in its heart because its heart is just behind your head. (Interview 8: Female, Pre-Family, Rural)

I believe in angels and I think we have all got a guardian angel... you can actually evoke your guardian angel to you and I think often you can feel the presence as well. (Interview 58: Female, Late Family, Suburban City)

Interestingly, even those people who had no time for angels as spiritual beings were quite willing to appropriate the term and, as it were, secularise it for their own purposes.

Not so sure about floaty things with big wings but I believe there are people on this earth whose lives are probably very similar to an angel. (Interview 52: Female, Late Family, Suburban City)

In one curious story a clearly human individual was interpreted as an angel, with a conclusion that was curiously traditional given the respondent's own lack of faith.

Once in the shape of a tramp, another extraordinary story… It was a tramp about 15 years ago who we met at some mission thing in Leamington. We were chatting to him and the following day I saw him camping out by the railway station in the centre of town. It was late autumn and was quite cold and I remember saying to him "Do you want to come back to our house". He said yes and we went back and we went to the mission and as a result of going to that mission, the second night actually, our daughter on that occasion sort of responded to what the speaker was saying and she became a Christian that night, so it felt like he was…[sent]. Yes, that sort of angel. (Interview 35: Female, Empty Nester, Suburban Town)

One respondent, who rejected their existence, recognised the significance of angels for the human mind and in doing so made perhaps the most perceptive single comment about them.

I don't think there are any but they fill a very good spot in our minds and vocabulary. We all know what an angel is, lovely word, no need to explain that. [It's] very seldom if ever misused, angel of mercy and all that. Good word and influence. (Interview 11: Male, Empty Nester, Rural)

Prayer and **meditation**, two areas that might have been interpreted as quite distinct entities, were perceived as relatively similar. There were some differences, meditation being more about me and prayer being primarily about petition, yet these were less evident than their similarity.

Meditation was understood positively, although with some uncertainty. It was commonly seen to be about reconnecting with your 'essence' or 'inner self' or 'innate nature'.

Very important going back to finding out who you are. It might just even be cooking by yourself. (Interview 7: Female, Student, Rural)

I practise meditation all the time because to me it is the way of getting or aligning you with your higher self. (Interview 8: Female, Pre-Family, Rural)

It was something that elevated and relaxed you.

Higher state of being or a state of grace. (Interview 10: Male, Late Family, Rural)

It's a kind of deep relaxation. (Interview 61: Female, Late Family/ Empty Nester, Urban City)

It was something that, therefore, did not need to be 'spiritual'.

Meditation I don't think has anything spiritual about it. It is just a way of clarifying your brain in order to help you think about things clearly. (Interview 44: Male, Pre-Family, Suburban Town)

Prayer was also spoken of positively, for similar reasons.

Prayer is a quiet time for yourself, to air your views or to talk. (Interview 2: Male, Pre-Family, Rural)

I think it does kind of work because I have read how it kind of refreshes your mind. You think of something really beautiful and amazing and if you focus on that it makes you feel good and happy. (Interview 43: Female, Student, Suburban Town)

Its effect was comforting and strengthening.

I do feel it has brought me quite a lot of comfort and strength. (Interview 17: Female, Empty Nester, Rural)

I think you can get a lot of comfort out of prayer if you think about what you are saying and you are in the right place. I don't say it has to be in church. (Interview 48: Female, Widowed, Suburban Town)

The important thing about prayer (as we shall see clearly in the responses to more directly ecclesiastical issues) was that it had to be on my terms. You do not need to go to church to pray.

[I] don't see [the] need to go to church even if they believe in God. Can still pray elsewhere. (Interview 50: Female, Pre-Family, Suburban City)

I don't believe prayer has to be done in any particular type of building. (Interview 49: Male, Student, Suburban City)

Nor should prayer be about what you *should* say. It should come from the heart.

Now I only pray when I need help, which sounds very selfish. (Interview 13: Female, Student, Rural)

Being able to say whatever is in my mind and my life, knowing full well that he is not going to turn his back. (Interview 52: Female, Late Family, Suburban City)

It is worth noting that one respondent who recognised the petitionary nature of prayer did so in such a way as secularised the word, in much the same way as 'angel' could be used as a deliberately non-spiritual term. Prayer, in this instance, is essentially a kind of hope.

Some things I might hope to myself but more of a wish or hope rather than a prayer. (Interview 45: Female, Early Family, Suburban Town)

The final issue, **miracles**, was a commonly used term but one that, like angel and prayer but even more so, had been widely secularised. When respondents spoke of miracles, there was little sense of the laws of nature being broken. Indeed some respondents explicitly denied such possibilities, usually because they hadn't seen them or because by definition they could not happen.

I've heard lots of stories about miracles. Me, I wouldn't be able to accept it until I see it. (Interview 37: Male, Student, Suburban Town)

Miracle is something that is impossible to be happening in the world. (Interview 33: Male, Early Family, Suburban Town)

When such miracles do appear to happen, it is simply because we don't understand the workings of the universe sufficiently well.

What I do know is that the universe is immensely complex and we strive towards an understanding of how it works and as far as I can see every time we reach a new understanding what it does is open further doors to which we don't understand. What I would say is that if something which appears to be a miracle appears it is simply something we don't yet understand. (Interview 34: Male, Late Family, Suburban Town)

Something that appears to be impossible but might not necessarily be within the confines of what our understanding is. (Interview 56: Male, Early Family, Suburban City)

There were a handful of respondents, it should be mentioned, who did appear to interpret miracles in the traditional sense and believed in them too, although expressing such belief in less rigorous terms.

I think there are many people around on this planet that are performing miracles, in relation to hands-on healing, people who have been diagnosed with cancer for instance and have been given by the orthodox profession two or three months to live and 15 years later they are still going strong and the cancer has completely gone. (Interview 58: Female, Late Family, Suburban City)

More common was the modernised reinterpretation (and popular usage) of 'miracle', as perceptively outlined by one student.

It depends how you define it. In the way that it is described in the Bible, say you are terminally ill and suddenly getting better, I wouldn't say it is a miracle. There must be something inside that has made them get better. I think the word is overused. I think when people say it is a miracle that I got here because the traffic was so heavy, that is not a miracle. (Interview 43: Female, Student, Suburban Town)

This example, of arriving on time despite heavy traffic, was well chosen. Some examples offered bordered on the trite.

I was driving along to work one day and a lorry threw a concrete block over my car, which landed on the bonnet of the car behind me. Now I think that must have been a miracle, basically for the fact that if it had landed on me I wouldn't be here. So I think somebody was watching out for me. (Interview 39: Female, Early Family, Suburban Town)

There were plenty of examples of people using the word miracle to mean 'lucky' in this way.

If a building collapsed and everybody is pronounced dead and a little baby child is found. It was meant to happen. That is a miracle because that baby was meant to survive. (Interview 2: Male, Pre-Family, Rural)

I've been in the one [church] where.... You see that was a miracle. That bomb dropped and went straight through the roof of the cathedral, landed in the middle of the floor of the church and it never exploded. (Interview 48: Female, Widowed, Suburban Town)

When someone has been very ill and somehow become better. Also when people come out of a very bad accident. (Interview 6: Female, Widowed, Rural)

Miracle was also used as a near synonym for awe. There were numerous respondents who said that:

The human brain is a miracle. (Interview 3: Male, Early Family, Rural)

My kids, I think, are miracles. (Interview 21: Female, Early Family, Urban City)

How life happens is a miracle. (Interview 16: Male, Late Family, Rural)

The miracle of things coming up every year, flowers, trees etc that is a miracle to me. (Interview 24: Female, Widowed, Urban City)

These five areas – ghosts, angels, prayer, meditation, and miracles – were, therefore, more immediate and relevant to a greater proportion of respondents, although this did not mean that they had any tangible impact on them. Conspicuous by its absence was any sense that believing in or experiencing these various things had made any major difference to people's lives. The only consistent reaction was that there was a lesson to keep one's mind open.

Not to have a closed mind but to be open-minded and not to assume that I know it all and that there are other things going on around you and to respect it. (Interview 3: Male, Early Family, Rural)

It has made me realise that there is a lot more to flesh and blood and physicalness. (Interview 56: Male, Early Family, Suburban City)

Probably to realise that things are more complex than you first believe. It is easy to go by day-to-day life without really thinking about things or listening to yourself or emotions and it is not until you go into these places that it is sort of special. (Interview 7: Female, Student, Rural)

Three other facts about people's attitude to a spiritual reality should be noted. The first is the general lack of pattern of who did and did not believe in such a reality. If anything, a positive response was more characteristic of the young, which is to say not so much that older respondents reacted more negatively but that their spiritual attitudes were shaped slightly more by the Christianity of the culture in which they had grown up. They might have similar attitudes to spirituality but it was more recognisably, though by no means, Christian. This balance does, as observed, correspond with broader quantitative surveys on the topic but should be taken as indicative rather than definitive in this instance.

Similarly, there was a relatively even balance between sexes and across geographical areas, of those who embraced, rejected and were hesitant about a supernatural realm, and no obvious life stage or lifestyle correlation as an explanation for their attitudes.

Secondly, there was an overall messiness to responses. The analysis above has given a vague structure to people's responses but it is important to emphasise that, although there were some respondents who were clearly deeply into the 'spiritual realm' and others who rejected everything (apart, possibly, from the existence of alien life) as hocus-pocus, the majority expressed views which, in as far as it is possible to tell, were complex, confused, contradictory, or chaotic. No respondent had anything approaching a system or ordered set of presuppositions or beliefs through which they could interpret what they felt, thought, believed and experienced. The result was something of a smorgasbord of half-thought out, sometimes deeply-felt, sometimes easily-dismissed, reports, feelings and opinions.

The third and final point is the fact that reasonably intelligent, comfortable, well-educated and articulate as many of these respondents were, there was a willingness among most, though by no means all, to credit the *possibility* of a spiritual realm. The number of respondents who instantly slammed the door on the very idea was very small indeed. Even the most sceptical respondent of all those interviewed had this to say:

A very close friend of ours, Chris, had a powerful experience of oneness with the universe. He's now a Methodist lay preacher as Christianity offered the best, not complete, explanation for this. He's very intellectual....it has made me take this kind of thing much more seriously and to recognize it as something which is real, not for me perhaps but for other people. It was because Chris is very intelligent and an academic and not the sort of person to make that kind of thing up. (Interview 34: Male, Late Family, Suburban Town)

6. Questions about Suffering

People often like to complain in surveys. It is very easy to point out the sins of the world. It feels cathartic and can even offer a sense of well being for sounding so socially concerned. Analysis must factor this in. Just because people say things are rotten, it doesn't mean they are. If people were *really* concerned about the state of affairs in which they live they would do more about it than surveys show they do.

That said, it is wrong (not to mention arrogant) to ignore their criticisms on these grounds. The question of suffering was central to a number of respondents and its overall importance was reflected in what all interviewees said about the state of the nation and of the world.

Even after factoring in respondents' natural negativity, interviews registered a broad and comprehensive range of concerns, and these, as will be seen in section two, have an impact on their attitude to and relationship with Christianity and the Church.

6.1 Areas of concern

It is often difficult to disentangle people's areas of concern – *what* they are concerned about – from the perceived reasons – *why* they are worried about them. The two are, after all, very closely linked. There will inevitably, therefore, be a degree of overlap between this section and the next.

Broadly speaking concerns fell into three categories: personal, national and international.

Personal concerns were obvious and ubiquitous. Everyone had experienced or known someone who had experienced some personal loss, a fact that sometimes emerged during and affected the discussion of whether or not the universe was planned.

Of the national concerns, some form of **social breakdown** was the greatest worry, although this could take a number of forms. The most extreme was **violent crime**.

I am glad I am not long for this world because I would go mad at all the things that are happening... you get someone else with a gun shooting down the road... this weekend. Three incidents down Sewell Highway. (Interview 30: Female, Separated, Urban City)

More prosaically and more pervasively there was the general problem of **anti-social behaviour**.

There were some children tonight on the television, eight year olds, destroyed a cemetery. Playing in a cemetery, smashed all the stones, pulled all the flowers out. That's not right is it? I wouldn't have dared do anything like that when I was eight and my kiddies wouldn't have done at eight. (Interview 48: Female, Widowed, Suburban Town)

Interestingly, although older respondents expressed these concerns most frequently, a number of younger respondents felt the same way.

The youth around here nowadays, the parents have got no discipline and that could be really bad in the future for this area. You have got all these young kids, age 11 or 12 and they are already trying to steal cars. (Interview 19: Male, Student, Urban City)

How society has fragmented itself almost into little cliques that don't sit comfortably with me. It hasn't changed for the better – the increase in anti-social behaviour and that is so broad so I will sum it up as that. (Interview 27: Female, Early/Late Family, Urban City)

Directly tied in with this concern with the behaviour of young people in society, was the sense that **the law** was either powerless or inept in dealing with situations as they merited.

I cannot understand the way the law is with just standard crime like burglary etc. (Interview 15: Female, Early Family, Rural)

I am concerned that the criminals are winning. We don't seem to have any way of beating the criminals. The police seem to have their hands tied behind them. (Interview 47: Male, Empty Nester, Suburban Town)

I sometimes feel that they [children] ... don't get the right punishment, but perhaps that isn't the right way to look at it. I don't think they are punished properly. (Interview 48: Female, Widowed, Suburban Town)

The **breakdown of the family** was a particular cause for concern, although it was often just as much a *reason* for other problems as a problem in itself.

You might think I am a bit of a prude but I sit here and I see these girls with cigarettes in their mouth pushing their babies and think "Why should they be kept by this state?" They should be married first before they have babies... these girls get pregnant so that they can get a flat and won't have to work, and that is my firm belief. I had to go to work to keep my children and I wasn't an unmarried mother – I was a deserted wife and nobody helped me. (Interview 30: Female, Separated, Urban City)

A separate but frequently mentioned problem was that of asylum seekers, popularly perceived as exploiting the state.

I am very concerned about how we let lots of people in… we have got to be the easiest country who lets everybody in… When they get here we look after them very well, almost putting the British residents to the back of the queue with regard to hospitals, interviews and things like that. (Interview 15: Female, Early Family, Rural)

The trouble is that it is getting a very mixed race in here now. It may blow up soon with the asylum seekers, because you have got people wanting houses and they can't get them, but they see asylum seekers getting properties and I think that could cause a problem in the long run. (Interview 23: Male, Empty Nester, Urban City)

In the international arena there were, broadly speaking, five areas of concern. **America** was mentioned by a number of particularly younger respondents.

Internationally it is the fascist mega-power of America and they have set their sights on us. They are bullying. (Interview 38: Male, Pre-Family, Suburban Town)

America causes me concern. They have got far too much power than they should have. America concerns me because it is a bit too big for its own boots… I am all into conspiracy theories. I do think America's own government killed JFK for whatever reason. I do think they took Martin Luther King out as well because they were frightened of something and the power these people had and they didn't like it. (Interview 26: Male, Pre-Family, Urban City)

Secondly, there was the **environment** and the ongoing damage humans are doing to it.

No rain forests left, that is a real big problem. There might be drugs out there in those plants that we don't know about that might do good in the future. (Interview 39: Female, Early Family, Suburban Town)

Thirdly, there was the spread of **AIDS**, woefully ignored by Western governments.

AIDS situation... governments are spending loads of money on arms, guns and things, yet the help they could be providing for people in Africa is unbelievable... drug companies that are making vast amount of profits out of people's miseries. (Interview 29: Female, Empty Nester, Urban City)

Fourthly, there were the dangers of **globalisation** and its impact (or lack of it) on global poverty.

I don't like big commercial organisations and the way these global companies seem to take over the world. The Murdochs, Microsofts of this world... What I don't like is the profit motive being about all and everything. (Interview 18: Male, Widowed, Rural)

Result of globalisation... I was reading one day in the newspaper that well over 50% of people live on less than a dollar a day. (Interview 37: Male, Student, Suburban Town)

Finally, a number of respondents mentioned**religion** as an area of concern, particularly in the way it breeds resentment and violence.

I do not like the way religion seems to be causing more and more conflict throughout the world and the Muslims worry me

a lot! I can't get my head around the way they think.
(Interview 18: Male, Widowed, Rural)

6.2 The reasons

Asking respondents who or what they thought was responsible for these problems tapped a rich vein. Reasons, primarily for the more immediate, national concerns, flooded out, ranging from deeply personal explanations to wholly structural ones.

There was a lack of **discipline** and guidance that started problems early.

The discipline has slowly over the years relaxed. I think it has gone too far, I really do. (Interview 52: Female, Late Family, Suburban City)

It starts with tiny children; they have no guidance. I don't mean rules and regulations and beatings but just guidance. (Interview 24: Female, Widowed, Urban City)

I see a lot of people abusing drink... extremely intelligent young people who just throw it all away because they want to go out and have a good time... I see young people ruining their lives through pregnancy. (Interview 13: Female, Student, Rural)

In a similar vein, there was concern for a lack of **respect**. These explanations were more popular among older respondents (as one would expect) but by no means absent from younger ones.

Where has the respect for one another gone? It doesn't matter how young or how old, it's just this rivalry with one another. I think we have become very materialistic and it is all about what we have got and not what we have to give to other people. (Interview 49: Male, Student, Suburban City)

The respect has gone. When I was a child you respected people and other people's property... your father's look was enough. I was more frightened of my father finding out than the policeman finding out. (Interview 53: Female, Empty Nester, Suburban City)

Breakdown of **community** and **trust** were closely linked to these factors, again voiced by young and old respondents alike.

People these days are not as friendly as they used to be. In my younger days here it used to be open house. You knew all your neighbours and you never locked your doors. You were in contact with them more. Today you are lucky if you speak to your neighbour, once in six months. There is not that community spirit like it used to be. (Interview 53: Female, Empty Nester, Suburban City)

People don't trust any more, they're loath to trust one another. (Interview 49: Male, Student, Suburban City)

In the bungalow this week you can hear the kids out at 11pm at night screaming. What are they doing out at that time of night? When I come back late at night you see youngsters around, like the other week I was coming down the Ansty road by the Mount Pleasant at 1.30am in the morning and there were 14 or 15 youngsters out all dressed up. That is the problem. It is not the parents' fault, it is always somebody else's fault – no one is taking responsibility. (Interview 23: Male, Empty Nester, Urban City)

Accompanying these points, there is a culture of **blame** and **victim-hood**.

People believe that everything is always someone else's fault. Society seems to be breeding people, my children included, who have no sense of responsibility and that is going to cause massive problems in the future. (Interview 9: Female, Early Family, Rural)

A handful of respondents, more commonly rural ones, blamed **ignorance** or a lack of **education** or **reflection.**

Lack of education... which is society's fault. (Interview 7: Female, Student, Rural)

A lack of serious reflection of what they are and who they are themselves... a lot of people's lives these days are spent trying to avoid those fundamental truths. (Interview 10: Male, Late Family, Rural)

Perhaps most significantly there was a sense that **materialism** dominated and distorted society now.

We are all materialistic and I wonder when does there come a point where it is saturated. It is a throwaway society. People are constantly throwing things away whereas our parents kept things for life. (Interview 45: Female, Early Family, Suburban Town)

In the civilised world it has got so selfish and self-centred. We don't care about other people's plight, like people affected by floods or AIDS in Africa because we would rather go and get a new car or something. (Interview 40: Male, Late Family, Suburban Town)

As these comments suggest, it wasn't just materialism that was at fault but the culture it encouraged. It was a culture of **instant gratification**.

A lot of youngsters – well, it is not all youngsters and crime. They can't be bothered to save up and buy something – they want it now. (Interview 28: Female, Empty Nester, Urban City)

There was a culture of **perpetual material dissatisfaction.**

I think once you start earning money you feel like you deserve it and then maybe you want more and are never happy with your position. You always want to move up the hierarchy. Your desire will always defeat your actual beliefs. (Interview 44: Male, Pre-Family, Suburban Town)

The people who are starting to make money want to make more money. It's normally people in influential positions and they do it because it's become an obsession – it's almost like an addiction. (Interview 3: Male, Early Family, Rural)

There was a culture of acceptable **greed** that displaced people and relationships.

Margaret Thatcher – she started it in this country... a lot of it needed doing but it was the attitude that came through which she started, this attitude of having more all the time. (Interview 40: Male, Late Family, Suburban Town)

People today have different values and standards. They are more for the material things in life and not in a communal spirit. (Interview 53: Female, Empty Nester, Suburban City)

Don't you think a relationship would be much more worthwhile than struggling to make money? (Interview 36: Female, Widowed, Suburban Town)

These, then, are the main perceived reasons for current social problems: greed, materialism, ignorance and a lack of discipline, guidance, respect and community spirit. Such comments were interesting in the way they pointed the finger at people in general rather than simply scapegoating members of society.

There was, however, a fair amount of that too. As already mentioned, **asylum seekers** were blamed for many social problems, often because they were perceived to benefit at the expense of others. The issues provoked real anger on occasions.

Why has this man been moved from his country of origin, say, for example, Kosovo and then been housed in Coventry, which... the local authority furnishes? Most people have to go to work to buy a cooker, yet this guy has it given him... If I joined the housing list in my last town that I lived in I had a wait of 12/13 year for a flat... I have seen it first hand where local authorities have given these people kitchen appliances such as cookers, washing machines and even a TV. Why they need a bloody TV I don't know because the job centre does not advertise jobs on the TV... I expect to go to work to earn money to buy things. It is the fact that these people are treated differently and we have to work for it. (Interview 26: Male, Pre-Family, Urban City)

I feel sorry for the Asylum Seekers but I still don't think this country should take them. We take too many... I can understand people complaining about people coming to this country when we can't help ourselves – it's very difficult. (Interview 53: Female, Empty Nester, Suburban City)

I think it is because of all the people coming into the country. I am not against them coming in, but they swing the lead when they arrive and get money handouts. Why should they get handouts, when I have had to work for them all my life? (Interview 42: Male, Widowed, Suburban Town)

More generally, **'religion'** and 'religious people' were at fault, largely because they were to blame for 'most wars'.

Religion as well... because a lot of the stuff in Iraq is over that. (Interview 51: Female, Early Family, Suburban City)

Interestingly, those respondents who expanded on this point sometimes betrayed their own prejudices. Religion was to blame even when it patently wasn't. For example:

Religion. I think a lot of it is religion. I mean look at Hitler, he wanted to get rid of all the Jews. Then there are the Arabs, they think they are right, we think we are right. (Interview 48: Female, Widowed, Suburban Town)

The Jews and the Arabs have been fighting since biblical times and they are still at it. What causes that? I still put religion at the base of it. (Interview 18: Male, Widowed, Rural)

In actual fact, for religion most people actually meant aggressive intolerance of other people's belief systems.

Religion or people's intolerance of other people's religion... It is not necessarily RELIGION, capital letters, but the fact the people of different faiths or different religions find it impossible to live side by side. Greed for land, greed for tribal factions. Again I think the word is intolerance from anybody else who has a different belief, colour or way of looking at life. (Interview 17: Female, Empty Nester, Rural)

A third category of people to blame was those in **power**. People in power were deemed to act unilaterally, arrogantly, carelessly, insincerely, or simply to abuse their power. Again, the proximity to the Iraq war clearly shaped opinions.

I suppose the government taking everything into their own hands and not consulting us. It is probably more so America's government rather than ours. (Interview 20: Female, Pre-Family, Urban City)

Part of it is politics and not understanding other people's views and not being prepared to listen in some cases. The closed-mind attitude really. (Interview 45: Female, Early Family, Suburban Town)

There was, however, a strange muteness in many of these criticisms. Given how fashionable it is to blame politicians for everything, there was an unusual absence of venom in many criticisms. Indeed, the paucity of comments and the tone of resignation with which some respondents spoke suggested that there was a sense that politicians whilst being culpable of some sins, could not fairly be blamed for all the problems around them.

There was widespread criticism for a group of people loosely called '**do-gooders**'. These comments came almost exclusively from older respondents and more from urban than rural respondents. 'Do-gooders' or 'liberals' were accused of encouraging disrespect and anti-social behaviour, albeit sometimes unconsciously and with the best of motives, by their refusal to discipline children, punish criminals, protect social order and enforce the rule of law.

I think there are too many do-gooders. They want to do good in the wrong kind of ways. I think softly softly doesn't work at all. (Interview 29: Female, Empty Nester, Urban City)

The general consensus was that their admirable ideas went 'too far'.

I certainly don't admire these so called do-gooders because I think they do more harm than good. (Interview 60: Male, Widowed, Suburban City)

I think that is taken a bit too far sometimes. I think sometimes the do-gooders go a bit too far. I know they are there to watch over and everything, but sometimes I think they go too far. (Interview 6: Female, Widowed, Rural)

The detrimental impact of 'do-gooders' was also associated with the lack of role-models available to children and also to the more general lack of standards. It also elicited sympathy for teachers and situations they had to deal with.

I don't think people nowadays have got the role models which they used to have years ago. (Interview 29: Female, Empty Nester, Urban City)

The liberal society – do-gooders who think it is a good idea not to punish the child. Parents do the same thing. I don't know who is to blame. Some people blame the establishment, but I think it is a decline in standards all the way round. The school staff can't discipline them now, they dare not do anything or you have the parents banging on the door. (Interview 23: Male, Empty Nester, Urban City)

Finally among the scapegoats, there was the **media**. Its all-pervasive influence did not lend it to specific criticism but it was generally blamed for exposing and implicitly condoning a dehumanising culture of violence and disrespect. Of all the finger-pointing criticisms, this was least limited to older respondents.

People weren't disciplined from an early age... too much crime on the television. (Interview 15: Female, Early Family, Rural)

I think a lot of violence, I am quite convinced, is because of what we see on the TV and films. (Interview 54: Female, Widowed, Suburban City)

6.3 What can be done about it?

Given the extent and breadth of the concerns, notably few people had cogent suggestions about how to address them. This partly reflects the fact that problems are more readily expressed in research than solutions, and partly the sense that many problems, serious as they were, felt a long way from home.

As a general rule, the more urban the respondent, the more likely he or she was to have experienced the problems about which they complained, though there was no direct correlation in this. The sample was too small to tell whether this sense of immediacy corresponded to an interviewee's activism, but such activism was, in any case, very infrequent.

A small handful of respondents saw absolutely no link between their local scene and the problems they had been discussing but they were the exception. Not surprisingly these tended to be rural respondents.

The local scene I believe to be... completely separate to what I would consider to be worldly affairs. (Interview 4: Male, Late Family, Rural)

It doesn't [affect me] in the slightest. That is about the most saving grace. I think village life to me is a stabilizing factor in my life. (Interview 18: Male, Widowed, Rural)

More often there was some weak link, such as in the number of charity shops in the locality, the 'Britishness' of the population, or more seriously, in experiences of crime.

There is quite a lot of families around this estate who actually believe in violence and also you do see a bit of poverty around here as well, so I think once again it is the way they have been brought up and the way they are taught to react, but there is nothing to stop them or get help and to show them another way to live. (Interview 21: Female, Early Family, Urban City)

By far the commonest 'solution' to these problems was a slightly vague sense of the power of example, an attitude of 'I am doing my best by living a good life and I can only hope others will imitate me.'

I think [I make a difference] if I act in the way I want everyone to behave... if I try to influence the people around me... be a good influence. (Interview 1: Female, Student, Rural)

I am just a grain of sand. I do my best to affect the people around me, family, friends, as many people as I can. But I don't go out of my way to try to affect other people but I will try and help and not walk by. (Interview 56: Male, Early Family, Suburban City)

At the moment through my job with the children I work with, hopefully to try and... teach them standards, respect, self-respect and manners. (Interview 52: Female, Late Family, Suburban City)

Others said they did their bit by recycling, donating to charity shops and such things.

I do do a lot of recycling which certainly helps mother earth and the planet, doesn't it? (Interview 58: Female, Late Family, Suburban City)

A few younger respondents registered the desire to 'go out' and help when they got the chance, 'going out' usually meaning abroad.

I think often it is down to people like us... when people go out, you know, all these gap [year] projects. It's wonderful that people are going out there and actually helping... I think every individual can do something to help. (Interview 37: Male, Student, Suburban Town)

Two or three respondents could talk about personally engaging with local politics or campaigning in a committed or on-going way.

[It] is reflected just looking at your local council and what is going on, which is why I am a member of the Labour party because I think that I have a voice of what is happening on a local level. I am quite politically active, especially in Lower Stoke in Coventry because I feel that is my way of having a voice. It is no good moaning about things if you don't try to do something about them, which you can do on a local level... For me I suppose you can only start at grass roots level, because that is the only way you have some say on what is going on and hope that eventually it will go upwards. It will probably take a long time. Also by supporting people who are making a difference higher up, by perhaps filling in a petition or signing up to give money, contributing on a grass roots level. (Interview 22: Female, Late Family, Urban City)

I have stood as councillor before and would do so again because I am local and I know a lot of people and they know me. The thing is I don't have as much time now. (Interview 40: Male, Late Family, Suburban Town)

For the most part, however, people tended to express a sense of futility about their ability to make a difference.

I don't think that an individual like myself can influence it in any way. (Interview 2: Male, Pre-Family, Rural)

I used to vote but I have been so disillusioned over the years I just abstain... If someone asked me now who my MP was for this area, I couldn't tell them because I haven't got a clue. (Interview 29: Female, Empty Nester, Urban City)

I think we can all do small bits to make a difference but it is all small drops in the bucket. (Interview 35: Female, Empty Nester, Suburban Town)

What, then, did respondents think was the likely long-term outcome? Were things likely to get better or worse?

By and large, responses were negative. The heart of the issue was, according to a number of people, that a liberal society such as ours precluded any substantive agreement or unity and this effectively inhibited much action. (It is worth noting that this sentiment was often voiced by younger respondents, when it might be thought more natural to come from an older respondent).

I think the problem is that people are so diverse – you can't please all of the people so the smaller the colony or the village the more likely it is for people to work together and sustain some workable community. On the scale of 60 million people it is impossible. (Interview 44: Male, Pre-Family, Suburban Town)

I think it is physically impossible to get everyone to be coming from the same angle on things on life, to the point of not conflicting with each other. (Interview 32: Female, Pre-Family, Suburban Town)

Expanding on this, several respondents made the point that if there was no real agreement on 'the good', let alone how to encourage or enforce it, anti-social behaviour was almost bound to flourish.

What I am saying is that half of them around here don't realise that what they are doing is wrong. So until they do nobody will approach them because they know it would be a waste of time and they would probably get it thrown back in their face. (Interview 21: Female, Early Family, Urban City)

Moreover, several respondents recognised the negative impact social pressure could have on good behaviour.

It is very hard when you are trying to instil values into somebody and then they go out into the real world and everyone else isn't doing it, so they think why should we. (Interview 9: Female, Early Family, Rural)

Finally (among the pessimists) there was the feeling that because so many problems were problems of 'the human heart' rather than structural problems with society, there was not much the government could do about it. Indeed government interference, particularly if it were 'politically correct', could make matters worse.

I don't think it can be from the government... I think if you bring in too much legislation it backfires on you in the sense that you get Asian or West Indian people getting jobs that they are not qualified for, purely because they are Asian or West

Indian... Everybody should get it on their own merits. (Interview 17: Female, Empty Nester, Rural)

It is worth noting in passing that although the comparative lack of scathing criticism of those in power was rather anomalous, the underlying sense that a lack of values was responsible for many social problems concurs with earlier quantitative surveys such as the Nestle Family Monitor 1999 study *Mapping Britain's Moral Values.*[1]

It would be wrong to suggest that respondents had no sense of hope or ideas for change. When such suggestions were made, they tended to reflect the nature of the problems themselves.

So, for some respondents the need was for more education, although this was not so much the historic call to banish ignorance as a more modern one of inculcating values. Education was often moral education. It was, by and large, a younger point of view.

We need to teach people. We need to re-educate people that certain things they have been led to believe are not right and that they are damaging themselves and the world. (Interview 1: Female, Student, Rural)

Only through education, before people get into that position [of social destruction]. They are encouraged to love, to give and to see other people's needs and to think of others. (Interview 3: Male, Early Family, Rural)

For some respondents this new kind of education was very explicit.

---

1   http://www.nestle.co.uk/about/familymonitor/

*The 3 Rs. Respect for self, respect for others and respon-
sibility... you can't respect yourself at the expense of others
and you can't expect people to respect you if you don't take
responsibility for your own actions. (Interview 38: Male, Pre-
Family, Suburban Town)*

This view naturally verged on a misty-eyed conservatism,
though, again, not necessarily among older respondents.

*I would like people to be more charitable and go back to more
old-fashioned values and look out for their friends, neighbours
and community. I would like the pace of life to be slightly
slower. (Interview 27: Female, Early/Late Family, Urban City)*

There was the call for a greater degree of localisation – we
should *'live in smaller, self-contained communities'* according
to one respondent *(Interview 38: Male, Pre-Family, Suburban
Town)* – and also for a greater control of media content, though
this was acknowledged as a tough choice.

*If you stop all the advertising on the TV and in magazines...
[but] people aren't going to stop advertising. Everybody could
make a conscious decision not to buy but they would be in the
minority. I mean one of the teachers at my school will not
have a television and I wonder how they cope, but her family
don't miss it. You have to be very strong. (Interview 45:
Female, Early Family, Suburban Town)*

Some respondents called for a greater degree of social order
through law enforcement.

*Sometimes I think we need more policing, I am convinced we
need more police. (Interview 54: Female, Widowed, Suburban
City)*

Structural answers were limited. Very few people thought social anxiety was a result of deprivation. The only answer in this area was from one respondent who suggested *realistically affordable housing*' as a solution *(Interview 40: Male, Late Family, Suburban Town)*. Indeed, it was more common to suggest that the opposite was needed.

We had some good times even though we had nothing. No car, no television, no washing machine, we used to have a wooden box. I think sometimes, some of these youngsters need to start off like that, really, and then they will value what they do finally get. (Interview 48: Female, Widowed, Suburban Town)

On the international scene, one interviewee called for *a bigger version of United Nations*' *(Interview 43: Female, Student, Suburban Town)* and another voiced the common 'governments should get together' view.

I think the governments throughout the world need to get together, and stop faffing about it. Although it does worry me that in some third world countries the governments are so corrupt that whatever happens things won't improve. The aid doesn't get through. (Interview 39: Female, Early Family, Suburban Town)

Even taking respondents' comments with a pinch of salt, the sense of negativity about the future was disturbing, and not limited to older or urban respondents.

It is getting worse and worse or it seems to be getting worse. (Interview 49: Male, Student, Suburban City)

I find it very scary out there considering how it was when I grew up and how it is now 25 years later. In another 25 years I hate to say it but we will probably have to have guns… I really hope not, but it is quite scary out there. (Interview 15: Female, Early Family, Rural)

That worries me; what society is going to be like in 15-20 years time. When you see how some parents speak to the children and it's coming through schools now; we are having problems with primary children. There are more and more primary exclusions coming through and that worries me. (Interview 23: Male, Empty Nester, Urban City)

Positive answers were notable for their vagueness. They tended to have little more to go on than a general sense that things will get better, that history is progression, that people are generally nice or that pessimism is unpleasant.

I think there is no point in feeling negative because it just generates more people to feel pessimistic. Things can be done and things are being done. (Interview 37: Male, Student, Suburban Town)

The vast majority of humanity are good, hearty people and somehow their energy is going to be enough for the forces of darkness to not succeed... People's consciousness is changing sufficiently for them to stand up and say they have had enough of this. (Interview 8: Female, Pre-Family, Rural)

If you look at history things have got by and large on average better. (Interview 34: Male, Late Family, Suburban Town)

Overall, respondents had a powerful sense that something was wrong. This emerged partly in the more metaphysical areas of the interviews, when 'suffering' was commonly mentioned as one of the big questions, or a barrier to faith in God, but it was more clearly and more interestingly seen in the concrete examples and explanations for the world's problems.

The number of respondents and the breadth of their answers counsel against oversimplified summaries. The problem was as much with the human heart as it was with global capitalism, as much with liberal do-gooders as religious fanatics.

In as far as there was any single, over-arching explanation for suffering, it was not so much rooted in sin or personified evil but, more generally, in the exercise of our individual freedom that made living together difficult. Money, or more accurately materialism, corrupted relationships and values, and in place of the trust, respect and discipline that society needed, it fostered a culture of rights, blame and material gratification. Religion, or the narrow-minded and intolerant mindset it bred merely added to the troubles.

Section B

Attitudes to Christianity, Christians and the Church

Is Christianity the answer?

The short answer to this question was 'no': respondents did not feel that Christianity has the answers to life's big questions.

Given that none of the respondents were Christians (in any meaningful sense of the word) this is not wholly surprising. Recruitment criteria were such that those who might possibly have answered yes to this question were excluded. Respondents were typical of the sizeable proportion of the population that had moved out of the Christian mainstream while maintaining some of its beliefs.

Furthermore, respondents were not asked directly whether they thought Christianity provided the answer to the questions they had, and interviews did not have the bipartite structure that marks the analysis in this report. Interviewers asked respondents about their understanding of and attitudes towards Christianity and the Church but never tried to forge a link between their big questions and the answers of faith.

That caveat noted, it was still apparent that respondents found it difficult to envisage a significant link between their big questions and Christianity. Christianity, quite apart from being tarred with the brush of 'religion', was a distinct entity, self-contained and with little bearing on the things that matter to me, the one exception being found in the Church's role in community and society.

Although one must be careful about drawing conclusions from this – the interviews did not directly probe the possible link between the two – the research suggests a real need to articulate the relevance of Christianity in terms and concepts that people can understand.

This section looks at the attitude to some basic Christian teachings, exploring people's understanding and attitude, before moving on to the issue of the Church. Many of the findings echo and detail commonly acknowledged facts concerning people's understanding and opinion of religion, Christianity and the Church.

1. Who is Jesus?

Discussions about Jesus followed those about God in the flow of the interviews, with respondents talking about their general opinion of him, before responding to the crucifixion (with the aid of a picture) and saying whether they thought Jesus had made a difference to the world.

In research conducted by LICC in 2002 into the barriers and bridges to faith today, one young man claimed that:

Jesus was not a person. He's a made up character in the theatre... [the Bible is] probably just a book written by a silly old man who thought, "oh, this would be good." (Male, 18-24, London)

Such deliberate perversity and obtuseness was largely absent from *Beyond the Fringe* although one respondent (from the other end of the age spectrum) did say, *'I don't think he existed if I am honest' (Interview 48: Female, Widowed, Suburban Town)*. A few respondents said they thought Jesus was simply an 'ordinary bloke' whose life story had been exaggerated.

Jesus did exist, but I don't believe he was the Son of God and I don't think he did everything he is meant to have done... an ordinary guy with some interesting ideas. (Interview 1: Female, Student, Rural)

Somebody who really kind of sacrificed himself for everybody else. I think he was a normal type of guy and he tried to get people to listen to him. (Interview 39: Female, Early Family, Suburban Town)

One respondent did make the silent link between Jesus the 'ordinary bloke' and the man who gathered followers around him and claimed to be the Messiah. The two did not sit comfortably with one another.

I am not convinced that Jesus was the Son of God. I think he could have been a very accomplished con man, somebody who managed to get people following him. (Interview 18: Male, Widowed, Rural)

Rather more common was the idea that he was an extraordinary person whose life story had been further exaggerated. The precise reason for his 'extraordinariness' varied. For some he was a rebel leader.

A very influential man. He carried a people's revolt against the Romans. He was probably one of the most amazing people in history. The legend got kind of emphasised. (Interview 7: Female, Student, Rural)

For others, he was simply a wise, humane and charismatic man.

I think Jesus was a very wise, charismatic, person. (Interview 5: Male, Empty Nester, Rural)

He obviously had some very special qualities in the things he did and the way he treated others. (Interview 45: Female, Early Family, Suburban Town)

For others, he was first and foremost a great teacher.

I would say he was a teacher who had some insight in what we would call divine knowledge and tried to pass that on as best he could. He was persecuted because of that. I am not sure whether I believe he rose from the dead, so in connection between Christ and God I would say he was a teacher. He probably wasn't the first of his kind and won't be the last. (Interview 38: Male, Pre-Family, Suburban Town)

For others still, he was a great prophet, although the actual meaning of the term was rather vague. Note, incidentally, in the first quotation below, the possessive 'ours'. It implies the attitude that says, 'I may not go to church, believe Jesus to be the son of God or have any sympathy with 'organised' Christianity but Jesus is still 'ours' as against 'their' Mohammed.'

Jesus or whatever name in other religions use the same sort of person....I mean the Muslims have got Mohammed, haven't they? It is very similar to ours. (Interview 23: Male, Empty Nester, Urban City)

Perhaps Jesus was one of the greatest prophets but there were others. Were they prophets sent by God, as in the man with the white beard, or was this person, someone who was enlightened by the experience they had? Realised the positive energy that they had and gave this to others. (Interview 56: Male, Early Family, Suburban City)

I don't know whether he is any more important in the scheme of things as the other prophets of other religions. (Interview 17: Female, Empty Nester, Rural)

He could even have been an (angelic) master, as in one interpretation that became increasingly peculiar as it proceeded.

I think that Jesus was one of the great masters. I can only say one of the great masters because I think there were a lot who came to this planet. I think that he came onto this planet to bring that message of love... I think Jesus was one of the great angelic masters who chose to reincarnate on this planet to bring that message. (Interview 58: Female, Late Family, Suburban City)

What was beyond question was that his life had been coloured and exaggerated by his followers, most particularly those individuals who went on to found 'the Church'.

I don't necessarily disbelieve that Jesus was around; there might have been a guy around called Jesus who was a good bloke, but I don't believe in all the other stuff in the Bible. (Interview 51: Female, Early Family, Suburban City)

He came to teach us to love one another. He gave lectures telling us to love one another... but the Church hasn't understood what Jesus said and has distorted it really badly for reasons of wanting power. Particularly at the beginning of the Catholic Church where they persecuted people expressing their Christianity outside the Church. (Interview 8: Female, Pre-Family, Rural)

There were some objections to the idea of Jesus being 'Son of God', a term considered arrogant for a man of such transparent goodness.

The Son of God – maybe that was a bit arrogant. I don't think he was special. Surely God created everybody equal so why is Jesus special? (Interview 44: Male, Pre-Family, Suburban Town)

He didn't claim to be the Son of God. That is interpretation. (Interview 34: Male, Late Family, Suburban Town)

On the few occasions that the Virgin Birth was mentioned, a social explanation was offered.

Since I have got older I think actually that Jesus did exist. I don't say his name was Jesus, but as a man he actually existed, and I think he was the illegitimate son of Mary. That is only my own personal belief because in those days you couldn't say you were pregnant; it wasn't accepted; you would have been stoned to death. (Interview 29: Female, Empty Nester, Urban City)

I believe Mary had been a naughty girl and Joseph was a very understanding man. (Interview 11: Male, Empty Nester, Rural)

Some respondents reckoned Jesus to be the ultimate, complete and whole human being, in a way that sounds highly unorthodox but is actually, albeit unconsciously, not too far from the New Testament's view of him.

I think Jesus reached "Christhood" which is the goal of every human being and the destiny of every human being, where you are as perfect as you can be within our understanding of the physical body, and he isn't the only one who has reached that. So he is the purest manifestation of God that has ever been. Not the only one but the most well known. (Interview 8: Female, Pre-Family, Rural)

I believe that a lot of people on earth have got close to God and I think he got closest... I think it is hardly likely that a third of the miracles attributed to him were done by him. But the ones that he did do were about helping people believe in God and themselves... He gave people faith – that is what he did. I believe he came and he was and still is the greatest influence on the world... I am talking as a Christian. One of the injustices that I hate is that he had to die to prove it all. That poor fellow, age 33. (Interview 11: Male, Empty Nester, Rural)

You have the ability to be the same as Jesus but you decide not to be. (Interview 49: Male, Student, Suburban City)

In amidst this vague consensus that Jesus was a great moral teacher there were respondents – from every life-stage – who unambiguously associated him with God.

He is part of God. He was sent to earth by God to try and make people believe and become more respectful to each other. (Interview 49: Male, Student, Suburban City)

I think the big one there is that maybe Jesus is the Son of God or maybe a representative of God, rather than the Son. (Interview 26: Male, Pre-Family, Urban City)

I think of them as one. Jesus and God as one. He is not a separate person. (Interview 53: Female, Empty Nester, Suburban City)

Such unambiguous association could sometimes come in the midst of other sceptical and confused interpretations.

He probably existed... He set an example to others.... You cannot talk about Jesus and not God. (Interview 50: Female, Pre-Family, Suburban City)

It is worth noting in passing two of the more extreme attitudes towards him, one from alleged personal experience and the second from an unspecified source. Again, it is worth noting the ability to believe in the absurd if it condemns the (Catholic) Church.

I was a little girl and I woke up one night and there was a man sitting on the side of my bed. I wasn't frightened and I have seen him a couple of times. He just sat there and I said to him "Who are you?" He said to me "You know who I am". I wasn't frightened and considering the only man in my family when I was a child was my brother you would think I would have been frightened – a strange man sitting on my bed – but I wasn't because I knew who he was. (Interview 36: Female, Widowed, Suburban Town)

Jesus had a family as far as I am concerned because he couldn't advise other people about bringing up a family if he hadn't experienced it himself. Mary Magdalene was his wife and he had a child with her along the Indian Line... There were seven popes in different parts of Europe and the person in charge decided that he wanted the Roman pope to have supremacy over the others but they didn't, so he was murdered and the emperor put in his own man to be pope and that is how

136

the Catholic church began, with murder. (Interview 8: Female, Pre-Family, Rural)

Given the variety of opinion of who Jesus was, there was reasonable consensus on what he was like. Even those respondents who rejected any theistic interpretation of his life, suggested, if only implicitly, that he was a good man. Commonly his name was associated with love.

I feel that I can connect to Jesus much more than I can to God because Jesus walked this earth, he was here, he actually lived. He's not sat on a throne eating bon bons... Jesus to me had unconditional love, from what I can gather, for everyone... Jesus to me was just a very compassionate man who was just there for everyone. (Interview 32: Female, Pre-Family, Suburban Town)

He sacrificed his life to basically benefit other people and to air his views in a way. (Interview 2: Male, Pre-Family, Rural)

I do believe, by the way, in a man called Jesus, perhaps not in the way that the churches do but I do believe there was a man who walked this earth called Jesus. I think he was trying to get over to people.... well, certainly the message was love, my goodness me, it is just that one word. (Interview 58: Female, Late Family, Suburban City)

Opinions of the crucifixion divided into two camps. Both recognised the horror of the event, but whereas the first left it at that, the second (much smaller) camp moved on to neutralise its obvious emotional impact by some form of rationalisation. There was some criticism of the 'he died for our sins' interpretation, motivated by incomprehension as much as anything else.

I always have difficulty in that 'he died to save us'. I always have difficulty with that. You know, he set us free by dying. I have never quite understood how he did that. (Interview 45: Female, Early Family, Suburban Town)

I do not view the crucifixion of Christ as a sacrifice. I don't believe in original sin and I don't believe he saved us all from hell. I think it is highly likely that a man who subsequently became to be called Jesus did historically exist and that he was a religious teacher. That is the establishment of the day, but in due course he suffered the all too common fate of subversive... I think it is possible that he didn't actually die at the crucifixion. After all there are other traditions that suggest a teacher very similar to him carried on elsewhere. Islam, for example, reveres somebody who sounds suspiciously like Jesus. (Interview 34: Male, Late Family, Suburban Town)

Another respondent remarked on the fact that the non-resistance of the cross merely acquiesced to evil.

I don't think he was a good Christian to be honest. I mean why did he lay down like that? I don't understand. What a waste. I don't think he did a good job. He saved us from our sins. Does that mean everyone since him hasn't gone to hell – I don't really understand? (Interview 44: Male, Pre-Family, Suburban Town)

Another interviewee rejected the idea of God doing that to his own son.

If that man hanging on that tree is God's son I don't want to know that God. How could he do that to his son? He to me was a man who suffered, agonised. No person or thing could do that to his son. (Interview 24: Female, Widowed, Urban City)

Implicit in these comments and, of course, in the wide belief in the exaggeration of biblical stories, was that the resurrection never happened.

I don't think that after his death he rose again and did more amazing things because it doesn't actually say that after he rose again anyone saw him. They saw this silhouette if you like of Jesus who came to help them, but I am sorry I have never seen him. (Interview 21: Female, Early Family, Urban City)

Only one respondent claimed otherwise, although even this belief in (the possibility of) the resurrection had little personal impact (in much the same way as those respondents who claimed to believe Jesus was the Son of God did nothing with their beliefs).

I think it [the resurrection] is probably very possible. If you believe enough in God and he was able to come as a human being then it is possible. (Interview 45: Female, Early Family, Suburban Town)

It should be fairly obvious, from the recruitment sample and from these comments about who Jesus was and what he did, that none of the respondents saw Jesus' impact on the world as anything to do with the power of the Holy Spirit or even as his role as God (when the phrase 'Son of God' was used by some respondents it was merely titular, rather than meaningful or descriptive). Instead, he had had a positive personal impact on people, partly through his example:

Very strong lessons in considering other people. (Interview 9: Female, Early Family, Rural)

And partly by offering them hope and purpose:

He's given a lot of people strength. (Interview 37: Male, Student, Suburban Town)

I think most people see his life as a guide and there is hope. (Interview 13: Female, Student, Rural)

It is human nature to be needed and wanted and to have a purpose and he has given that to them and that is an important thing. Probably not quite what he wanted, but maybe he did, but people take it too far and start hurting other people. (Interview 7: Female, Student, Rural)

This was sufficient for one respondent to say:

I think Jesus has been the biggest influence of good on the world that we have ever known. (Interview 11: Male, Empty Nester, Rural)

Other respondents – those who did not feel the need to vilify the Church at every opportunity – were positive about his impact as it had been transmitted through the Church.

There are a lot of Christians over the whole world and I think there are a lot more good people because they have followed the Christian faith. (Interview 39: Female, Early Family, Suburban Town)

He made you look at a person as a person... Also his religion that his friends started for him has lasted nearly 2000 years, so there must be a lot of good in it. (Interview 24: Female, Widowed, Urban City)

Lots of the law is based on Christian values and the commandments and things. Lots of people are against the [Iraq] war because of their religion. (Interview 43: Female, Student, Suburban Town)

Such comments were (more than) matched by ones that pointed out the Church's negative impact on the world but they were often reluctant to attribute that sin to Jesus. Note, incidentally, in the next quotation, the post-resurrection existence cited by this respondent and its similarity to one mentioned by respondent eight earlier.

He has certainly brought a message of love. I have to say unfortunately in relation to religion, Christian religion has been responsible for a lot of bloodshed over the years and still is. That is not Jesus' fault, but man's fault. I think when Jesus was on the cross, if Jesus was on the cross, I have to say that, because there is a serious role that he didn't die on the cross but he actually got married and had children. (Interview 58: Female, Late Family, Suburban City)

At a more personal level, several respondents said quite simply and honestly that he had had no effect on them whatsoever, a point that one young woman, whom we have already encountered, was quite passionate about. It was in these quotations that the implicit difference between the Jesus of history and the Christ of faith emerged.

I've been to church; for nine years I was made to go to church and sit there and believe and all that time I probably did believe but then he has done nothing for me to make me feel that yes he is up there and yes he does help people because I have never seen him help anyone yet... I do believe in him, I am not saying I don't but I don't think he is up there watching down on us, helping us, teaching us new things, whatever, I don't think he is all that. I think he was just a person who lived and is now dead. (Interview 21: Female, Early Family, Urban City)

The same respondent reiterated the point in her comments on the resurrection.

It is a bit far-fetched really isn't it? If you said to me, my aunt died the other day but when we pulled the coffin up three days later she had gone, you would automatically think that someone had nicked the body, wouldn't you? But they thought he had risen and was coming to save the world but he ain't come yet, has he? (Interview 21: Female, Early Family, Urban City)

Overall, Jesus emerged with a good reputation. He was unlikely to have been divine, and even if he were, there was no meaningful connection between his divinity and my humanity. Yet, among human beings, he was one of the very best, living and dying for love, wisdom and other people. In much the same way as prayer might be undertaken, not so much for its efficacy as for its psychological benefits, Jesus could be embraced for the sake of his example and inspiration rather than his divinity.

Every age, it has been observed, has the tendency to remodel Jesus in its own image. His goodness is so evident that almost no cause can afford to do without him and so he and his teachings are enlisted for a variety of causes. In these attitudes to Jesus we see a human being, a teacher, an individual, a courageous rebel, and a man touched by spiritual wisdom, whose life was brutally cut down by the authorities and then systematically misrepresented by a different set of authorities. It is to that 'misrepresentation' that we now turn.

2. What about the Bible?

The quantitative research survey that went into the BBC's programme 'What the world thinks of God' claimed to show that 42% of people in the UK had 'studied religious texts[1]. Anyone who has conducted more in-depth religious research among the British public will be surprised (to put it mildly) at that figure. However widely one interprets 'studying', it seems ludicrously inflated.

What it really shows is that 42% of Britons *believe* they have studied religious texts. In reality, this figure ties in closely with the 'inoculation' trend observed in LICC's *Beyond Belief?* study. This suggested that because Christianity (or more precisely a culturally accommodated version of it) has played such a major role in the forming of British culture and society, and because it remains there in the background of what we do, people have received a low-grade version of the real thing in such a way as has resulted in them becoming immune to the genuine article. Actual knowledge of Christianity is very limited but it is mistaken for genuine knowledge, causing people to become automatically resistant to the Gospel on the premise that they 'already know what it is all about'. We think we have studied religious texts (when really we did some RE at school and have a Bible somewhere at home), and so when we reject Christian claims we think we do so on the basis of informed consideration.

This came across in *Beyond the Fringe*. In spite of supposed textual study, any idea that it was 66 or so books rather than one (or at the most two), or that it was written over a time frame of centuries, was absent. Instead opinions as to what it

---

1   http://news.bbc.co.uk/1/hi/programmes/wtwtgod/default.stm

was fell into three distinct groups. Firstly, the Bible was an advice or rulebook of some kind.

A book of guidance... certainly the Old Testament was inspired by the Great Force to be written... I also feel that within the Bible there are a lot of things that instil fear into a lot of people. (Interview 58: Female, Late Family, Suburban City)

Within this category, one respondent described the Bible with an acronym that, as Christian acronyms go, is surely one of the best.

I would like to say that the Bible for me, B.I.B.L.E is a basic instruction book for life on earth. (Interview 56: Male, Early Family, Suburban City)

Second, it was a biography or history book, depending on whether you thought it was about Jesus or a bigger picture. Note, incidentally, in the second quotation the contrast between following the Bible and following 'your heart'. This, as much as any other comment, summarises the imagined transition between then and now. You either follow a book or your heart: you can't do both.

It is kind of like a "time line" of how the earth began with Adam and Eve and then in the New Testament how Jesus lived and what he was trying to teach people. (Interview 13: Female, Student, Rural)

Not so much a Holy Book, more as a very large diary of the events that happened when Jesus was around... I don't believe it is something that should be followed because I believe you should follow your heart, because there are a lot of things in there that are very contradictory. (Interview 49: Male, Student, Suburban City)

A history book of the world. (Interview 23: Male, Empty Nester, Urban City)

The belief that the Bible had been tampered with could be found in both of these categories.

I think it was their little book of rules, but obviously it has been embroidered and bits have been added and taken off. I think it was a rulebook for life. (Interview 29: Female, Empty Nester, Urban City)

Thirdly, it was a storybook, a term usually used primarily to undermine its veracity and reliability, rather than to describe its genre. For storybook you could sometimes read fairy-storybook. (Incidentally, the apparently bizarre, *non sequitur* comment that concludes the first quotation is used as a normative position by which the respondent judges and condemns the Bible.)

I am amazed how literally people take it and believe that there was an Adam and Eve and that the stones were literally burnt. I find that amazing... It's a moral tale of sorts. It is a parable and many parables have been written since, including soap operas and poets. It is not alone in that it portrays certain morals... There are lots of things that have been taken from the Bible and enforced and taken out of context. Surely God believes in free love? (Interview 44: Male, Pre-Family, Suburban Town)

It's got great stories for kids. I think the Bible is probably the story telling you the story of what happened... It has a moral, lessons to be learnt... I read Bible stories to my kids. (Interview 39: Female, Early Family, Suburban Town)

A lot of metaphors. I don't particularly believe that the world was created in seven days and all the rest of it; I just think it is a way of explaining in a way that we can understand about how the things came about. (Interview 32: Female, Pre-Family, Suburban Town)

I read some of it at school and remember quite enjoying it. I remember it more as a set of stories, fables. (Interview 38: Male, Pre-Family, Suburban Town)

Respondents' evaluations of the Bible were, not surprisingly, rather more negative than their evaluations of Jesus or of God. It was, as we have observed, condemned as being exaggerated and misremembered.

I think, I've heard that there is a lot of evidence to show that there are people like Jesus and his friends who lived in the place at the time and I think the Bible is based on them and then maybe exaggerated a bit. (Interview 43: Female, Student, Suburban Town)

In much the same way, it had been distorted by (mis)interpretation.

Obviously everything we know about what he [Jesus] is supposed to have done and said had been through a lot of hands before reaching us, so whose ulterior motive is it? ... A lot of people made a mistake when they wrote it down because [the] written word is subject to a lot of interpretation. If you don't understand something he said you interpret it in another way and as far as I know he didn't write anything down. There is a lot more to speech than actual words. It is the way you say it or body language or a number of other things going on. That makes all the difference. (Interview 38: Male, Pre-Family, Suburban Town)

The New Testament seems to have been written from memory by people who were there at the time... I am sure they wrote what they thought was the truth but as you can tell from the four gospels they are all interpreted differently. (Interview 24: Female, Widowed, Urban City)

At best, many of its stories were questionable.

It is something I can't work out whether it is true... like the parting of the water and the locusts, I can see how it happened but on a much smaller scale. I mean was there an earthquake or swarms of things? (Interview 61: Female, Late Family/ Empty Nester, Urban City)

At worst, they had simply been disproved.

I do sometimes question things when you see scientific viewpoints. I find that difficult for both of them to fit together... I sometimes think perhaps the Bible is wrong. (Interview 39: Female, Early Family, Suburban Town)

As a whole it was deemed full of contradictions.

I haven't got much time for the Bible. When I have read the Bible it is so contradictory and so... I just don't understand it... I have read the Bible myself. I find it contradictory and to be quite honest some of it is stupid as far as I am concerned. (Interview 30: Female, Separated, Urban City)

And perhaps most damningly, for some respondents it was simply irrelevant, although, at least in this example, not for the reasons you might expect.

You couldn't [live by it] in today's days. You couldn't use the Bible in its completeness like with the seven sins. You couldn't live like that now; you may have done in those days but not now... Like loving your neighbour. How could you love some of your neighbours? I mean be fair, some of them are awful and try as you might with all the patience in the world you couldn't love them. You may tolerate them but that is a totally different thing. There is no way you could love them. (Interview 29: Female, Empty Nester, Urban City)

That said it was not necessarily redundant. Some respondents had more positive attitudes towards it, though none revered it as Holy Scripture. A surprising number of respondents, and not simply older ones, lauded the Ten Commandments as a useful and important structure for social order.

I still think the strongest things in the world are the Ten Commandments, I really do. I am not a churchgoer but if everyone took notice of those commandments...that sounds rather pompous to say it, but things would be better. (Interview 45: Female, Early Family, Suburban Town)

If everyone followed the Ten Commandments we would be a lot better off. (Interview 56: Male, Early Family, Suburban City)

Another comment remarked on the emotional power of perhaps its most famous passage, although the quotation does not match up with the passage cited.

Psalm 23 is a song about good and evil and the battle between them. It is interesting because at the end they say, "Lord of Lord, King of Kings has returned to bring his children home and to take them to a New Jerusalem." That is the bit that makes me cry my eyes out because that is the bit that is a bit too close to home unfortunately. (Interview 26: Male, Pre-Family, Urban City)

Another interviewee made a similar remark, without the specific reference, and in doing so offered a small but interesting window on the nature of cultural Christianity, now almost entirely absent in younger generations.

I am glad the Bible is there. I never read from it myself. I love doing readings... in the church. I particularly like Harvest Festival because it is part of my life. (Interview 11: Male, Empty Nester, Rural)

Even those respondents who were eager to disparage its reliability and veracity felt that it could have its positive points. It was almost as if once it had been neutered it could be brought back into the fold, all fear of it impregnating minds with its false ideas gone.

I think it has a lot of truth in it but I don't believe it should be taken literally. (Interview 17: Female, Empty Nester, Rural)

[The] Old Testament is a compilation of the history and moral teachings of a particular eastern European, sorry, a particular tribe from Asia Minor, and the New Testament is, although it incorporates a history as well, it is much more to do with moral aspects. Don't get me wrong I am not saying the Bible is rubbish. There is a great deal of moral truth but unfortunately it also incorporates a great many things which encourages the more miserable minded to get involved with what other people would see as evil. (Interview 34: Male, Late Family, Suburban Town)

Overall, the Bible, insofar as it symbolised traditional, institutional religion was dismissed. Titbits of information were usually enough to convince people that the Bible was unreliable, self-contradictory or malign. This was by no means the unanimous opinion but it was the prevalent one, nourished by a profound ignorance of the Bible's contents.

However, once the Bible had been neutered – by being treated as 'just' a story, a series of metaphors, moral education for children, or some such moderately safe formula – it could be praised and indulged in. A deconstructed Bible, which allowed me to pick and choose and made fewer (or preferably no) demands on me, was an acceptable Bible.

3. Attitudes to Heaven and Hell

Respondents were also asked briefly about their attitudes to heaven and hell. Heaven was deemed, at least in theory, to be a nice idea.

I want to [believe in heaven...I'm] very confused about all that stuff to be honest. I want to and I really hope there is a heaven but there are certain parts of me that are not sure. (Interview 15: Female, Early Family, Rural)

It was also slightly absurd as an idea, at least in its traditional formulation.

I don't really believe in heaven and hell because I don't see how it is possible. The images you get, of like the pearly gates and sitting around on clouds, I don't see how it is possible. Likewise, hell, I can't imagine people living with loads of fire around them and stuff. (Interview 43: Female, Student, Suburban Town)

Its absurdity stemmed, at least in part, from people's inability to imagine anything convincing. Some people could only see the clichéd stereotype.

I don't think heaven is some pretty pastoral landscape where there is always fluffy white clouds and a nice blue sky and where all your ancestors and brothers float around you with white robes and wings and you spend your time telling God how wonderful he is... Apart from anything else it sounds incredibly boring. You frequently hear that all the interesting people go to Hell so that is where I want to go. (Interview 34: Male, Late Family, Suburban Town)

I just imagine it being all frothy with loads of clouds. Like marshmallow. (Interview 6: Female, Widowed, Rural)

A handful of other respondents were concerned with the space problem.

It must be an awfully crowded place if it does exist – wouldn't be able to move. (Interview 18: Male, Widowed, Rural)

I wonder where they put everybody. They have got to be in shadows, or ghosts because if they were all solid people there wouldn't be enough room up there. (Interview 42: Male, Widowed, Suburban Town)

Some people saw it as little more than a slightly better extension of earth.

Almost like you just carry on living like you are now. (Interview 31: Female, Student, Suburban Town)

I believe it is a place that on earth you have your most happiest moment. You are not just there with people who are there at that time, but you share it with everyone you love... Your warmest moments all rolled into one and you re-live them. (Interview 13: Female, Student, Rural)

In among these responses, there were some particularly charming ones.

Peace – no stress, no arguing, no. I always used to say I would go and weed his garden, but I was told that God doesn't have weeds in his garden, so I said I would just go and sit in it then. (Interview 36: Female, Widowed, Suburban Town)

Overall, the paucity of credible visions made believing in heaven difficult, although there was, not surprisingly, a wistful desire to believe. At least one respondent wanted assurance in order to 'believe' in it – and in doing so revealed a common confusion between faith and proof.

If it was proved to be true then I would believe in it, but right now I don't believe. (Interview 43: Female, Student, Suburban Town)

Hell, not surprisingly, was less popular. The idea of categorising or judging people was anathema.

I'm not sure about this thing about people being categorised. If you're good you'll go to heaven, if not it's hell. I don't think that somehow seems quite right. (Interview 37: Male, Student, Suburban Town)

I wouldn't imagine that God would punish you – would he? (Interview 15: Female, Early Family, Rural)

Yet, some people saw, on consideration, the merits in some form of judgement, although in these instances euphemism and inference reigned supreme. There was often a link in such responses to the idea discussed earlier that true wickedness was not in taking human life but abusing it. It is also worth noting that such a (very tentative) leaning towards (the possibility) of judgement and punishment was an all-age phenomenon.

I'd like to think that people who have committed crimes such as rape – I would like to think that there is a sort of hellish place for them to go. (Interview 2: Male, Pre-Family, Rural)

If you go around raping women and murdering them as Peter Sutcliffe did I don't think you actually believe you are going to get into heaven when you die and meet your maker. I do believe that the deeds you do do affect where you go. Perhaps there is a tally chart. (Interview 26: Male, Pre-Family, Urban City)

In a funny way I feel that if you were to do awful things I believe you may suffer in some way. (Interview 15: Female, Early Family, Rural)

I don't believe everyone goes to heaven. (Interview 4: Male, Late Family, Rural)

Only one respondent saw hell as a self-imposed state rather than a punishment.

It is not a punishment.... it is a self-imposed punishment. (Interview 8: Female, Pre-Family, Rural)

Several other respondents described it as a place of utter confinement, the logical concomitant to our deification of freedom.

[Hell is] the eternal prison sentence. (Interview 13: Female, Student, Rural)

I think that if you are in heaven you can sort of roam, but in hell you are more confined, like a prison cell. I think even hell might be still your spirit trapped inside your body and not allowed to come out of the body and have a free roam. (Interview 2: Male, Pre-Family, Rural)

Perhaps the biggest question about heaven and hell was whether they were simply manifestations of earth or not. Numerous respondents claimed that heaven and/or hell were here and now, either in actuality or in potential.

I think you should try to make heaven on earth. (Interview 51: Female, Early Family, Suburban City)

I think earth is heaven and we should make the best of it. (Interview 5: Male, Empty Nester, Rural)

Conversely, earth could indeed be hell itself.

I think you make your own hell here. (Interview 30: Female, Separated, Urban City)

I think there is so much hell in the world, why make some more when you go somewhere else? (Interview 17: Female, Empty Nester, Rural)

And two respondents, quite independently, described now as hell and death as heaven.

Hell is living and heaven when you die is calm. It is calm when you die. (Interview 28: Female, Empty Nester, Urban City)

I think sometimes that this is Hell and we go on to Heaven. (Interview 48: Female, Widowed, Suburban Town)

In effect, earth could be made into heaven or hell, a view that elbowed its way into the gap left by the clichéd and unimaginable heaven of tradition.

I don't believe everyone is going up to sit on clouds with angels and Jesus, and all the millions and millions of people who have lived on earth are all crammed into one space. I think there is heaven on earth and hell on earth. (Interview 17: Female, Empty Nester, Rural)

Only one respondent related the whole question back to the issue of human purpose.

There has got to be a better place than this because if there isn't there is no point in all your faith, all your beliefs. No point in anything if you struggle here all your life and then you die and there is nothing. (Interview 36: Female, Widowed, Suburban Town)

Overall, people's attitude to traditional (if not necessarily biblical) religious claims about heaven and hell was similar to their opinion of Jesus and the Bible. The orthodox view was rejected, although the ideas behind it were sometimes retained. Heaven and hell, rather like angels, may be unbelievable and rather childish concepts, but they are *useful* ones. As such, they can be appropriated as metaphors or examples but were rarely to be taken seriously.

The exception was when some respondents drew the link between the absolute morality they had discussed earlier in the interview and the idea of judgement. Hell was an abominable prospect but not necessarily more objectionable than rape or child abuse. In such circumstances, squeamishness and a subtle reluctance to use traditional terms (for fear that they might imply credulousness or naiveté) saw respondents using euphemisms wherever they could. Yet the idea of judgement implicit in serious moral thinking still remained in the shadows.

More notable was the fact that the majority of respondents did *not* make such a link. Far more were willing to engage in the idea and seriousness of absolute morality than they were in the concept of heaven or hell, an indication of the disjunction between the big questions of purpose, morality and destiny which usually lurk somewhere in people's minds, and the historically formulated religious responses to them. The two were, for all intents and purposes, operating in distinct spheres.

4. Any answers in church?

The Church is an institution and institutions are not popular today. The fact that the Church's image is poor and that church attendance is falling fast in comparison to broader religious and spiritual beliefs is widely recognised This research project supported these (and various other) well-established conclusions about the role and status of the Church in British society, and while these points will be mentioned in the analysis, effort has been made not simply to rehash the long-recognised criticisms of the Church being irrelevant and boring, and Christianity being antiquated and inflexible.

Instead, there is more focus on the reason why answers were (thought) not to be found in church.

4.1 Experience of church

As one would expect, experience of church was varied (bearing in mind that the selection process tended to act as a filter on fulfilling and positive experiences). Those positive experiences that were mentioned spoke of a church that was welcoming, connected to real life, lively and energetic, and that offered a sense of worth and belonging. They came from respondents of all ages. The words used – 'worthy, love, understanding, communicate, freely, share, support, peace' – are excellent examples of what people aspire to in such a relationship and of the vocabulary they use to describe it.

If I go into a Church of England church I feel completely worthy and welcome, I guess. (Interview 13: Female, Student, Rural)

A place full of love and understanding where people can communicate freely and to share the happiness and sorrows and get support when needed. (Interview 33: Male, Early Family, Suburban Town)

When I used to go to church at Braunston I used to go to the early communion at 8am because there was no music at all, and when I came away I felt good, peaceful and glad that I went. (Interview 48: Female, Widowed, Suburban Town)

Those with positive experiences were well aware that it was not necessarily like that.

If it is somewhere like St. John's with banners up and is quite modern, has a real vibe about it and has people my own age, then it is connected with normal society. Then great, it makes me feel elated, alive and there's a real energy and a loving atmosphere. But often you go into places, orthodox churches or whatever, and they are beautiful buildings, but boring. (Interview 32: Female, Pre-Family, Suburban Town)

Can be fantastic and really energetic and full of life and love. But it can also be thoroughly boring and tends to be non-connecting to the real world. Sadly the latter is how people perceive it, whether that is right or not. (Interview 32: Female, Pre-Family, Suburban Town)

Negative experiences were, of course, rather more common, partly because of the sample and partly because criticising the Church is a popular pastime today. Some negative experiences were not really *experiences* at all but merely recitations of public criticism.

If you go back to how people use power I think there has been corruption within the Church and through the media it has been well highlighted... I think the top of the Church are corrupt. *(Interview 56: Male, Early Family, Suburban City)*

Other opinions were more heartfelt and poignant and were a synthesis of bad personal experience and a general atmosphere of anti-religious feeling. The following quotation is a long but interesting example of an individual on a spiritual quest, who, having moved away from Christianity, felt unlikely to return and certainly wanted nothing to do with the Church that is, according to her views, shallow, glib and bigoted.

For about five years I have looked for spiritual direction. My inquisitiveness and my search still goes on but I am not hell bent on trying to find answers. I am just waiting... as time goes on I don't want to go back into the Church and cannot embrace Christianity as I did before. It feels completely wrong and I can't embrace Christianity, but who knows? One thing I am absolutely sure about is that I could not and would not want to embrace the Church, its narrowness. I think it is very bigoted. I don't think the Church is willing to look at very important grey areas in life. I don't think it is truly willing to look at the very painful areas like homosexuality, sexuality, sin and evil that lie within us but it is also this idea that we are all sinners in a rather glib sort of way. These are such heavy labels and I think it is far less straightforward that we are just sinners and need cleansing... I start to distrust a lot of things and can't trust the outright black and white statements that are made and on which our faith is supposed to be based. (Interview 35: Female, Empty Nester, Suburban Town)

The same respondent also came up with one of the finest soundbites in the research, here put in bold.

I think there are certain flaws with the established Church in that it is patriarchal and is built on rites and rituals. It has so *much dogma that **I think the established Church could be tried in a court of justice and could be found guilty of killing off spirituality**. (Interview 35: Female, Empty Nester, Suburban Town)*

4.2 Perceived problems with the Church

Overall, all the criticisms (and abuse) in the book were levelled at the Church: it was dull, narrow, bigoted, hypocritical, embarrassing, unreal, prescriptive, unspiritual, judgemental, patriarchal, credulous, inflexible, corrupt, unnecessary, a waste of time, and unable to handle doubt.

Familiar as this list will be it is not much help to anyone who wants to do anything about it. It is more useful to look into experiences that provoked such attitudes and to note that broadly speaking they fell into seven categories.

Firstly, there was the experience of church as **dull** and **anodyne**.

A bit staid. It can be very traditional. It is predictable... it is boring and you are probably not listening to anything that is said or done. Just paying lip service, standing up and sitting down at the right time. It is just happening around you. (Interview 52: Female, Late Family, Suburban City)

It should be noted, in passing, that new forms of church did not have it all their own way.

The one thing about it is that I am not into what I call "Happy Clappy" side of things. I find that very difficult and this standing up in front of an audience and saying... I find that very embarrassing. You are talking about getting involved with people in a more modern way and there is something about the Church in that you need it to be old-fashioned in my point of view. (Interview 45: Female, Early Family, Suburban Town)

Second, there were the specifically **unfriendly** experiences, sometimes consumer unfriendly, sometimes more traumatic.

My daughter was married in Braunston Church and when she had David, she wanted to have him christened there, and the vicar wouldn't let her... they lived in Daventry then. We were still living in Braunston. You see I don't like that. That is not right. (Interview 48: Female, Widowed, Suburban Town)

I used to go over to my local church in Stockingford. I was very much looking into spiritualism at that time. I have looked into a lot of things so in that way I am quite eclectic in my approach to things. My local vicar at the time came and knocked on my door and said that he hadn't seen me in church for some time. I said I am going down to the local spiritualist church because I am curious and he started preaching to me. I could see as he went out he stood in the door way and he held his Bible up like that and he said to me "You will rot in the fires of hell" and his Bible was going like that and he frightened me to death. (Interview 58: Female, Late Family, Suburban City)

Third, there was the sense, sometimes through experience, sometimes through reputation, that the Church was **hypocritical** and therefore forfeited its right to loyalty.

The fellow who christened me went off with the woman next door. He cleared off with the woman next door. I thought this religion is strange, they are all running to church but they are the biggest lot of hypocrites out. (Interview 30: Female, Separated, Urban City)

Fourth, there was a sense of **alienation** and **nervousness** that a poor welcome, explanation and integration bred. Even if this were not enough to drive someone from church, it was a powerful enough experience to shape a mindset.

We went to this pram service... they gave me the brass collection plate with a velvet cloth on and told me I had got to take the collection. So, well, I started and was so nervous. The cloth fell off mine. I picked it up but all the way down my side you could hear clang, clang, clang, so when I had finished and was ready to go down to the altar, I was trying to get the money on the top of this velvet. (Interview 48: Female, Widowed, Suburban Town)

Fifth, the experience of **inflexibility** and **absolutism** had driven some people away.

I was in the forces now, where we used to have the religious classes. I was one for asking questions and apparently in religion you are not supposed to do too much of that... Either you are a believer and if you start asking... well, I was called an atheist because I was asking too many questions. (Interview 60: Male, Widowed, Suburban City)

Within the church there is a constant scratching around or looking for some definite answers, finite reasons for things. I think it is very unrealistic. It is the sort of thinking that comes out of children and in a way it appeals to people out there who are finding life difficult. It is rubbish, because at the end of the day it is still a matter of faith. What the Church has done is say "We know this to be true". We can only say that we think we know it is true. The one thing that is not handled too well is doubt and uncertainty. (Interview 35: Female, Empty Nester, Suburban Town)

Sixth, slightly more broadly, there was the overwhelming sense that church was **unnecessary**. If, as many respondents felt, you could pray and relate to God without a church and outside any religious mainstream, what was the point of church? The section in bold in the second quotation ranks as one of the most pointed and representative soundbites of the entire research study.

It is a waste of time. I don't like the fact that you are sitting there for two hours talking about someone who might be made up. Those two hours you could have done some shopping or something useful. (Interview 19: Male, Student, Urban City)

*I said **I don't need the church because I have got God anyway**. I don't feel I need church... Jesus didn't meet in the church, did he? – he met in the house. (Interview 36: Female, Widowed, Suburban Town)*

Finally, there was a **rejection of the idea that spirituality should be the province of any one group**, let alone any one building or doctrine, a sentiment keenly voiced by the 'killing off spirituality' respondent. The following quotation and, in particular, her final sentence is an indictment of the disconnection between questions and answers that runs through this report.

I do believe that there is quite likely a spirit world and I quite believe that there might very well be a god or a power, but I think the kind of very prescriptive and very detailed interpretation of a Christian God and Jesus and Holy Spirit is the thing that I probably have a problem with and making it fit. It doesn't mean to say God doesn't exist. This comes round to the fact that I believe very strongly that we as human beings need to feel that we have got a relationship with somebody or something that is bigger and stronger than us. It is part of our

163

human nature. We have huge powers to generate what we want. The Church does not deal with stuff like that. (Interview 35: Female, Empty Nester, Suburban Town)

These general experiences of church compared interestingly with the specific reasons given for having left church. Some respondents had once been churchgoers and hence were able to describe why they no longer were. Of the four specific reasons for rejecting church, the first was its **failure to help in a time of need**. The lessons from this story are made very clear in the respondent's final sentence.

We lost our son. Church as a body of people basically were nowhere to be seen and we felt at the time that God had let us down, definitely... People we believed were friends were just nowhere. The church was nowhere and we were left... Maybe now looking back perhaps the people didn't know how to handle things like that. (Interview 52: Female, Late Family, Suburban City)

The second was as a result of general drift through a **change of circumstances**.

I was about 13/14 when I stopped going. I found that my friend used to go to places on a Sunday and she used to invite me along. I needed a bit of a break and then I met Alan and it just... like I say I don't feel that you have to go to church just to believe. I go now and again but not very often. (Interview 20: Female, Pre-Family, Urban City)

Third (and very honestly given people's usual unwillingness to admit its power), there was the **influence of peer pressure**.

[I used to go to] Christian Life Ministries... You used to play games and then sit down for an hour and talk about the Bible and stuff... twice a week. I used to go to the club and then the

Sunday service... I used to get the mick taken out of me and was called "Bible Basher". (Interview 20: Female, Pre-Family, Urban City)

Up until the age of ten I used to go with mum and dad every week. After that, they decided it was up to us to make up our own minds whether we wanted to go or not and I kind of did. I did for a while until I was about twelve and then I didn't. I think that was to do with peer pressure and it wasn't cool. When you are a teenager you desperately want to fit in and doing something religious is perceived, or you think it is perceived, as being a bit 'square'. (Interview 32: Female, Pre-Family, Suburban Town)

Finally, there was an example of **church being all consuming**.

If we could not make a meeting, a church meeting or whatever, it was dreadful, you couldn't have another life... so now I think that is why I don't get involved in a church now. (Interview 52: Female, Late Family, Suburban City)

None of these reasons was especially common (not surprising given the nature of the sample) but it is still worth noting how dissimilar they are to the general 'experiences' given above. In all probability, the two kinds of reasons work together so that general experiences (i.e. experiences filtered and shaped by broad reputation) pave the way for the rejection that personal experiences provoke.

One other, particularly moving story is worth noting, not so much as a reason for rejection but as a warning to those who peddle cheap grace and easy miracles.

We went before then every Sunday afternoon, because there is a Chinese community in the church centre and we went there to learn [the] Bible. On Christmas Day we went to a church in

Kenilworth. Just after praying, when we came out, Charmaine [my wife] hurt her leg just by the stairs and she was only four weeks to go to the due time for her baby and she was hurt. Nothing happened, and two days after she said she couldn't feel her baby. We went to the hospital and the baby was born by emergency caesarean, because it had lost ¾ of blood. That was because she was hurt in church... the effects caused the cerebral palsy. I do think God is not fair to us. I prayed many times on the way from home to Algarve but he had a blood transfusion twice. I cried many times. I looked down and said "God, if you want to punish me for anything I have done wrong, please don't punish my child." ... This is quite difficult for us. I mean if there is a God in the world; this tragedy happened to us in the eyes of God in the church. We would love to have the support and feel the love of God. (Interview 33: Male, Early Family, Suburban Town)

It is worth noting, in parenthesis, the various attitudes to cathedrals and church buildings. People spoke of both kinds of building positively, seeing them as spiritual, awe-inspiring, beautiful, calming, affecting buildings that could even help one's spirituality. Cathedrals were particularly praised.

I feel there are individuals and spirits around you that are looking over you in churches and cathedrals. (Interview 2: Male, Pre-Family, Rural)

I am a great fan of cathedrals. Whenever I am in a city and there is a big cathedral I always try and take a look at it. It is very humbling and it amazes me the effort they put in building them all those years ago. All the decades and lives. It amazes me how someone had so much belief in something that they spent so much time. Sometimes I think it is such a magnificent homage to pay to humanity that they built something so beautiful. (Interview 44: Male, Pre-Family, Suburban Town)

Old parish churches had the same effect.

When I walk into St. John's, like I said to you, I feel quite overwhelmed emotionally a lot of the time when I am there. But whether that's because of the love in there I don't know, I can't explain. It just happens. (Interview 32: Female, Pre-Family, Suburban Town)

It can be a refuge from the stresses of life. (Interview 23: Male, Empty Nester, Urban City)

Several older respondents, in particular, saw the church as an environment that helped prayer and had a positive impact on one's spiritual life. Unusually, for them surroundings *did* matter.

During our life we are always praying but when I go into a church and I pray, I feel that that is deeper. Do you know what I mean? (Interview 30: Female, Separated, Urban City)

I know it doesn't matter where you are and you can worship anywhere but surroundings help. (Interview 22: Female, Late Family, Urban City)

There were, however, some respondents who felt that churches were too serious, smelling of hierarchy and order.

They always come across in churches as being very very serious places, which is terrible really. Not that I am saying that they shouldn't be serious, but it is all too much dictatorship. It is not personal enough for me. I suppose not having been to church since probably the age of 16, I still have the feeling that it is all very regimental. (Interview 49: Male, Student, Suburban City)

I suppose [in] very orthodox churches it doesn't feel real. I cannot relate to that. It feels that you are worshipping something that is not there... Society has moved on so much, massively since Jesus was on this earth... it is totally irrelevant to most of my friends. (Interview 32: Female, Pre-Family, Suburban Town)

4.3 The Death of Christian Britain?

The surprisingly rich responses to the 70:7 ratio provided the confluence of many of these themes.

Respondents were 'shown' the 70:7 ratio – the fact that 70% of people call themselves Christian, yet only around 7% attend a church each week[1] – and asked why they thought this was so. Not only were there a large number of detailed and perceptive responses but many summarised the attitudes and opinions already expressed.

Firstly, there were reasons we have already met. Church is perceived to be boring, a chore, **too static**, and even morbid – a comment made across the board but more common among younger respondents.

I think people my age find it boring I guess in a sense; they don't see it as something they want to do on a Sunday morning. (Interview 13: Female, Student, Rural)

I broke this routine later on and I think that was because it was so much of a routine. It wasn't like enjoyable... sometimes it was a bit of a chore. (Interview 37: Male, Student, Suburban Town)

---

1 According to the 2001 Census and data from Christian Research respectively

Such comments often came with suggestions to make the experience more lively and interactive.

Moving around the church should be part if it. I see it far too static and restricting. Allow people to be themselves and to bring the natural things into the church. (Interview 8: Female, Pre-Family, Rural)

Second, there was the belief that church was **too didactic** and punitive, and insufficiently spiritual. Underlying this opinion was a belief that church was into 'control' and was there to tell people what to do, something which sits ill-at-ease with our culture's sometimes aggressive egalitarianism.

I kind of personally don't like being told what to think or what I should think. (Interview 31: Female, Student, Suburban Town)

This was such a negative element that even when a respondent recognised a church's other advantages, it could be a deciding factor. Being modern here is synonymous with openness and flexibility.

I think functionally religion is a good thing and it is good to surround yourself with people who believe in your beliefs and talk about it. Therefore church is a good thing but it doesn't offer that. It kind of tells you and you listen and go home. It is not very modern. (Interview 7: Female, Student, Rural)

Third, attending church, particularly as a stranger, can be **intimidating**. Although there is an element of hypothesising in such comments – a sense of intimidation is rarely a *sufficient* disincentive – it is true that the fear of intimidation can be that final source of friction that actually inhibits attendance. Regular churchgoers readily forget how strange and daunting attending a Sunday service can seem.

It might be quite intimidating going in if they are not believing on the same level as everyone else does. (Interview 31: Female, Student, Suburban Town)

If you were a newcomer and somebody got up and you didn't understand the words and things it could be a bit off-putting. (Interview 20: Female, Pre-Family, Urban City)

Because I am not a regular, and because they do these things like responses and things… I feel a bit stupid because they all know what they are doing and I haven't got a clue. Then all of a sudden they sort of start hugging each other, and I don't like that. I don't know them and I don't want strangers putting their arms around me and hugging me. (Interview 29: Female, Empty Nester, Urban City)

And if the ordinary, 'I don't know how they do things round here' feeling can be off-putting, more obvious forms of intimidation are unacceptable.

I find it incredibly offensive when he and other people say after a sermon "Now then, put your hands up if you have told somebody about God this week?" I say to [him], "How old are you? How ashamed do you want people to be?" (Interview 35: Female, Empty Nester, Suburban Town)

Fourth, there was a sense that the church is **out-of-touch**, partly in style but also in its mores.

People co-habit like Dave and I are doing. We are not sinners for doing that. We shouldn't be condemned for doing that. We love each other. Things and society change. I think the Church needs to change or numbers will dwindle more than they are doing now. (Interview 32: Female, Pre-Family, Suburban Town)

These four reasons were grounded in what the Church was (perceived to be) doing or doing wrong. In effect, the form of its 'answers' – its style, tone, worship, format – failed to make contact with where people were and with what they wanted.

Part of the reason why most people don't go to church is because it doesn't really connect with what they understand and what is said is not really meaningful to them... Worshipping God should be joyful. There is not a lot of joy in the Church. You are allowed to sing, but most of these are Victorian, down and depressing words. Some of the tunes are, yet some of the Taize chants do create joy. (Interview 8: Female, Pre-Family, Rural)

In a similar way, one respondent neatly epitomised the way in which there was a disconnection between the Church's 'answers' and the bigger picture of people's lives. Christianity had drifted away from questions of spirituality and life and was occupying an isolated theological ghetto (emphasis added).

I don't think that in this day and age people want religion rammed down their throats. **They want it as part of a bigger picture**, *can you understand that? (Interview 29: Female, Empty Nester, Urban City)*

Respondents also recognised that this disconnection was due, at least in part, to society. A fifth answer to the 70:7 ratio was that society is more **anti-institutional**. People don't go to church because it is an institution and nothing good can come from an institution.

I think people are more sceptical about institutions like the Church (Interview 7: Female, Student, Rural)

In a similar way, in spite of all the positive noises we make about community, society remains subtly **anti-community** today. As Leslie Paul wrote in a report of the future of the Church as long ago as 1964, churches cannot be part of what no longer exists.

When we were young and went to church on Sunday mornings, the church was packed. But we were such a small village community. [The church is empty today] because other people come in [to the village] and they don't go [to church]. (Interview 6: Female, Widowed, Rural)

By far the two commonest explanations, however, were that going to church was **unnecessary** and that people today are **too busy**.

It was in the first of these answers that we saw the separation of Christianity and spirituality most clearly. It came across the ages, sexes and socio-economic groups. Time and again the implicit question in respondents' answers was *what was Church for?*

I think if you feel the need to pray and worship you don't need to go to a church and if you believe in God you must believe that he is everywhere and can hear you so you don't need to go to a church. (Interview 1: Female, Student, Rural)

You don't have to be there if he is everywhere. (Interview 9: Female, Early Family, Rural)

They don't see belief in God and going to church as being necessarily automatically linked. (Interview 34: Male, Late Family, Suburban Town)

Within this there was an implicit reaction against the idea that going to church made you into a Christian.

I heard a saying fairly recently that standing in a garage makes you no more a car than going to church makes you a Christian. (Interview 10: Male, Late Family, Rural)

The other reason, that people are too busy, was the single most frequently cited explanation. Whether it is because of work, TV or family commitments, people have other things to be doing, with the implication that other things are more important or worthwhile.

Television.   People have got more to distract them and entertain them depending on your point of view. Busy lives. It used to be a family event with people getting dressed up and going to church. The idea of dressing up and going to church implies it is a social occasion. Now generally people live alone; the only explanation is that they can be entertained with films etc in their own home. (Interview 44: Male, Pre-Family, Suburban Town)

At the moment I don't go because it is on a Sunday and that is part of my weekend. I know that sounds a silly excuse but I am usually doing something else. The church I used to go to has become very un-dynamic and also not so many of my peers go to church, so I feel no desire to go. (Interview 22: Female, Late Family, Urban City)

I think there are lots of other things to do these days, lots of freedoms and entertainments. (Interview 5: Male, Empty Nester, Rural)

Weekend working was a particular constraint.

Work has taken over. You have to go to work for so many hours a week to be able to live in society, leaving you very stressed and tired at weekends and sometimes even working weekends as well, especially Robert.   He works 1 in 3

Saturdays and occasionally has to do the odd Sunday. (Interview 15: Female, Early Family, Rural)

I think the trouble is in the last 10 years the life-style of people has changed. Shops are open on a Sunday and it is a seven-day-a-week culture. Some people are working six days a week, so Sunday is the only day to go shopping and do other things. Sometimes the service times are awkward, either 8 am in the morning or 11.45 am when they are preparing meals. Also evensong is an awkward time so that could be the problem. It is not conforming. If people want to go other times in the week it is not available because the church is locked up. (Interview 23: Male, Empty Nester, Urban City)

In among these comments were some that claimed that the people themselves were not necessarily victims but were themselves lazy.

Because in the main people are lazy and society is encouraging laziness and convenience. The church expects you to put yourself out and 90% of the people don't want to put themselves out. (Interview 3: Male, Early Family, Rural)

Can't be bothered and that is it... If they are like me, they come home at weekends after working, spend the weekend cleaning, washing and ironing and they can't be bothered. It is awful because it is only an hour because I have said that myself. You should do it and I feel you should... Because you are showing you appreciate... making a physical effort to show you appreciate your life. You should physically find that time. It is one of those things that I will do when I get older. (Interview 45: Female, Early Family, Suburban Town)

Just can't be bothered to go. In this day of TV and videos they would rather stay at home. (Interview 28: Female, Empty Nester, Urban City)

These two critical reasons for the Church's failure to connect – its (perceived) irrelevance to its audience and its audience's (perceived) all-consuming busyness – were captured neatly in one comment which comes as close as any to summarising the general concensus of opinion.

You can pray in the garden but you can't do the gardening in a church. (Interview 52: Female, Late Family, Suburban City)

At the end of the day, gardening (or its equivalent in other lives) was not only more malleable to my schedule and also perhaps more enjoyable, but could also be just as spiritual. Why go to Church if you can meet God in your garden?

Section C

The Disconnection between People and Christianity

Using religious research can be a tricky affair. On the one hand, following respondents' advice is usually the fastest and most effective way of emptying churches and of draining Christianity of its meaning and distinctiveness. During LICC's research project *Beyond Belief?,* one respondent remarked (entirely without irony) that for the Church to appeal to people today it needed to *'knock the cross down – make it more modern, user friendly. Take that church bit away from it.' (Male, 25-44, London).* Although there was no advice quite like this in *Beyond the Fringe*, the general nature of responses often pointed in that direction. People's natural inclination is to remake the Church in their own image and when that image is shaped by the culture in which they live, as it invariably is, the Church suffers.

On the other hand, it is pointless, not to mention arrogant, to listen carefully to the often heartfelt sentiments of so many people only to ignore them because we believe we already know what's best. Doing so is usually the second fastest and most effective way of emptying churches, making Christianity appear alien, unsympathetic and irrelevant.

Instead, a careful balancing act is demanded. People's opinions should be used to shape not the Christian message itself but the way in which it is embodied in and communicated to an unfamiliar culture. This can be done by locating and using genuine 'contact points', by employing language that connects with rather than alienates people, by developing worship and liturgy that inspires rather than bemuses participants, and by telling stories that enthuse rather than bore listeners.

Beyond the Fringe suggests that this is a fruitful and necessary exercise. It reminds us of the breadth, depth, complexity, and unpredictability of spirituality today. It confirms other research that has shown that the demise of religion has not meant the demise of spirituality: indeed, quite the opposite. People like to consider themselves spiritually motivated and have as many big questions they want answering as they ever did. Although the force of these is dulled by materialism, they refuse to disappear. What happens after we die? Why are we here? How should we live? What is wrong with the world? What can be done about it? Does God exist? Does he have any relevance to my life? Is there a spiritual realm? Such questions lie beneath the surface of people's lives, of (supposedly) secular, 'post-Christian' young lives just as much as more traditional, 'late Christian' old ones. Occasionally they intrude directly into those lives. When they do and people search for 'meaning' or for the 'something there' that they have long sensed, they should feel as if they can turn to the Christian faith (even if it is only one option among many) for serious, meaningful responses. All too often, they do not.

The reason for this is not, of course, that the Christian faith fails to offer answers to these questions. In its own way, the gospel answers each, and not simply with a factual response, but with well-testified evidence, profoundly moving stories and, indeed, a living, global community. The real problem is that many elements of these responses no longer connect with a society that has changed enormously in only fifty years.

178

This final section offers a series of tentative reactions to this disconnection - suggestions that begin to point in the direction of the fuller, more considered responses that are detailed in the other publications and resources that accompany this research report (see Accompanying Resources page 10). In particular, they should be read in the light of and used as a signpost towards *Evangelism in a Spiritual Age: communicating faith in a changing culture* and *Equipping Your Church in a Spiritual Age*, rather than a substitute for them.

The Christian destiny

Even among the small minority of respondents who quickly dismissed the idea of an afterlife with a nihilistic sweep of the hand, there was often a desire for something more from life, a sense that it would be 'nice' if there were some kind of existence after death. This feeling was, not surprisingly, stronger among those more positively disposed to the idea of eternal destiny.

Neither group, however, was particularly clear about what this might entail, finding the options available unconvincing. Their confusion and incomprehension calls for several layers of engagement.

Firstly, there is an opportunity (and a need) to talk honestly about the reality and inevitability of death and to emphasise that a life lived in the shadow of death is both more realistic and more rewarding than one that buries its head in the sand and pretends that we will be here forever. Death puts life in perspective.

Second, there is a need to counter the 'here-is-all-we-have' mentality, which can often breed desperation or carelessness towards other people and future generations. The peculiar

Christian balance that sees the here and now as hugely important and yet dwarfed by the significance of eternity with God is a difficult one to strike, yet liberating when struck.

Third, there is a need to explain the coherence of evolution and possibility of an after-life. The fact that many Christians are perceived as reading Genesis 1 literally exacerbates this problem. Evolution tends to be an immoveable object in people's intellectual universes although this rarely stretches to the rather more dubious metaphysical conclusions espoused by some of the high priests of Darwinian atheism (i.e. that life is meaningless, directionless, purposeless, etc). People's sense that there must be more to life is simply too strong. That said, whilst evolution is relatively easy to grasp, comprehension of a credible afterlife is not, and this means that people's powerful sense of 'something else' often remains little more than an amorphous, personalised and inconclusive feeling.

Finally, there is widespread confusion between spiritualised, Platonic ideas and biblical ones, a confusion that can corrode or distort belief in an afterlife. This calls for two particular points of clarification: between the Platonic and biblical ideas of the soul (the one a ghost imprisoned in the flesh, the other the whole person in need of God) and between Platonic and biblical ideas of an afterlife (the one of liberated souls, the other of resurrected beings). Clarifying these ideas, whilst not being easy, would help to return to popular Christianity its unique and biting responses to the universal(ly popular) question of destiny.

A sense of purpose

The tensions inherent in respondents' thinking about purpose afford two significant contact points for the Christian faith.

Firstly, as noted above, respondents did not claim that life has a purpose but invariably lived as if it did. This needs pointing out, not so as to puncture people's false humility but to make them realise that to be human is to have some sense of purpose, no matter how vague, ill-defined or unsure that may be. When people recognise that their lives have a purpose, whether they like it or not, the question of what that purpose should be – should I live for myself, for others, for God, for the moment, for tomorrow, for heaven, etc? – becomes more concrete and immediate.

Second, the tension that ran through many respondents' attitudes was that whilst their sense of purpose was directed towards themselves (fulfilling my life, my potential, etc), it was also shaped by a profound admiration for those people who had done just the opposite and were prepared to sacrifice their goals and even themselves for other people. This tension is hard to reconcile, unless one embraces a worldview in which self-fulfilment is achieved through self-sacrifice, one in which, by loving others, we fulfil our potential and develop our humanity. Christ's promise of 'life to the full' combined with his challenge to 'deny [ourselves] and take up [our] cross' perfectly epitomises this worldview and reconciles this tension.

Engaging with creation

Respondents' attitude to and engagement with the rest of the created order offers two potential points of contact.

Firstly, the universal sense of awe is important. To be human, it seems, is to be awed. Not only is this the potential source of important, thought-provoking questions – why are we awed? why do we have this pervasive sense of the sacred? –but it offers real opportunity in worship. The respondent who remarked that the Church 'could be tried in a court of justice *and could be found guilty of killing off spirituality'* was speaking on behalf of many, albeit in rather aggressive terms. The opportunity for worship to tap into people's natural reservoirs of 'awe' is significant.

Second, in the same way as respondents repudiated the idea of their life having a purpose but lived as if they had one nonetheless, the fact that some respondents rejected the idea that life has a plan could not disguise the fact that they lived as if it did have one. Although this is not to suggest that determinism of any kind is a suitable or fruitful contact point for people, it is to recognise that we commonly make plans for our lives, live life as if we have a narrative, and retrospectively view our lives as if they were planned. The importance of narrative to the Christian faith has been much remarked on over recent years, with post-modernism placing real weight on the concept of narrative and highlighting Jesus' use of powerful stories throughout his ministry. Encouraging people to locate and articulate the sense of story in their lives, in a way that precludes immediate judgement, is a potentially fruitful exercise, inclining them towards a faith that is founded on an all-inclusive story.

The point of prayer

Given the fact that respondents' ideas about prayer were confused and the God to whom prayer was directed was at best unfamiliar and at worst highly dubious, there was a surprising amount of 'prayer' going on. Respondents' concepts of prayer, however, were often either hazy or limited to the petition or the cry of desperation. Meditation and contemplation were more readily associated with 'eastern' faiths than with Christianity.

There is a need, therefore, to explore the different 'types of prayer' or, more generally, the means by which we connect with God (or allow him to connect with us). The long history of Christian spirituality (see, for example, Bradley Holt's *A Brief History of Christian Spirituality*) provides a great resource in this area but there is, perhaps, a greater need to provide practical examples and workshops, and to teach people that prayer is not simply about asking God for things and that meditation is not simply an 'eastern' phenomenon but that both have a valid role in a rounded, Christian relationship with God.

When an individual can say, *'there have been a few times when I have felt that I have been connected to something bigger than myself... just for a split second,'* there is an obvious and important point of contact, if it can be explored sensitively and intelligently.

A counter-cultural community

As observed, respondents expressed genuine concern about the problem of suffering but this problem touched their lives not, primarily, as a difficult, theoretical question but through the problems and tragedies they encountered daily in their own lives and through the media. As noted, greed, materialism, ignorance and a lack of discipline, guidance, respect, and community spirit were perceived to be the main reasons for domestic social problems.

There is enormous opportunity for the Church to act as a counter-cultural community in response to this; a community in which such socially-corrosive trends have not taken root; a place where the values are relational – with each other, with God, with the rest of creation – rather than commercial; an arena in which people can operate as human beings rather than consumers; and a forum in which people may discuss and pray through their problems.

This response must, of course, begin with the Church itself. LICC's *Imagine* project (see www.licc.org.uk/articles/article. php/id/68 for details) explores how disciple making is key in the Church's attempt to reach the UK and evaluates, by means of a questionnaire, what are the key areas in which Christians need help. They are (in order of importance):

-   **life at home**, including how to be a good parent, how to maintain an appropriate home/work balance, how to support family and friends in an appropriate way, how to develop and maintain a loving marriage, and how to cope with loneliness and isolation

-   **health and security**, including how to deal with ill-heath and disability, how to cope with the death or sickness of a close family member, how to support ageing relatives, and how to manage personal finances, in particular, debts

-   **the workplace**, specifically the need for practical help and guidance in how to live as a Christian in a pressurized environment

-   **life in the church**, specifically relationships with a leadership that was either overbearing and heavy-handed or non-existent and 'fuzzy'

-   **personal spiritual life**, specifically 'the four Ds': direction ('hearing God' and 'receiving guidance'), discipline (living one's faith in a manic and sometimes hostile culture), handling doubt, and finally actually 'doing it' (e.g. how do I *use* personal, spiritual gifts? how do private spiritual disciplines actually go on to affect how I live?)

The *Imagine* research showed that whilst people were reasonably happy with the general quality of their church's teaching and preaching, they were commonly unhappy with its failure to connect with the issues they faced daily. People wanted relationship skills and training, *applied* biblical teaching, and information, knowledge and wisdom about 'current affairs, social and moral issues', so that they might be able to *live* their faith where they were.

This presents churches with the opportunity and challenge to offer training in a wide range of areas, many of which will connect with non-Christians in a way that a conventional Sunday service might not. Whether courses and workshops covered money-management, dealing with debt, work-life integration, bereavement counselling, or marriage and parenting guidance, churches could and should become arenas in which people develop the skills that enable them to live kingdom lives and help others to do likewise.

Mind your language

One of central themes of the *Beyond the Fringe* research was the disconnection between people's questions and the answers they perceived the Christian faith to offer. For the various reasons outlined above, this disconnection was inevitable and, thus, not an entirely fair criticism. That said, it did still point to an important truth that although people 'do theology' by nature (albeit often a godless theology) when they ask questions about destiny, purpose, suffering, creation, and spirituality, they are not aware of it.

Often this is due to an ignorance of the Christian faith but that ignorance is at least in part because Christian language (both spoken and enacted in liturgy, ritual, worship, etc) increasingly acts as a barrier to rather than a conveyor of meaning.

The concept of 'sin' is as good an example of this as any. Sin is, of course, central to the gospel, yet today the word sounds archaic, exclusive or simply meaningless. Not only does it not communicate what it should, about our moral, relational and directional nature as human beings, but it conveys a sense of institutional bullying, self-righteous hectoring and irrelevant, long-dead, petty-minded interference into people's lives. As one respondent from LICC's *Beyond Belief?* research said when describing (her understanding of) Christianity, *'He died on the cross and took on the sins of everybody. Sins being? God knows what a sin is, 'cos I don't to be honest.'*

The solution, however, is not to abandon the idea of sin, so as to make the gospel more 'accessible'. Rather, this dissonance demands a sensitive translation policy. For some people even this would make no difference: if you genuinely 'don't believe that there is such a thing as right or wrong', no amount of translation will make a difference. Yet, as *Beyond the Fringe* showed, not only did most respondents have a genuine sense of right and wrong but many had a rather useful word for moral failings: abuse.

That concept of abuse is profoundly Christian. The idea of 'abuse' only makes sense if one has some idea of the right and proper use of an object or person. It literally means use that has moved away from what it should be. In this way, the word comes very close to the true Christian understanding of sin as the corruption of a good relationship. Whilst 'sin' is now commonly either misunderstood by or incomprehensible to many people, 'abuse' is a familiar, better understood and personally meaningful term. 'Saving us from our sins' can sound alien and irrelevant 'Healing us from and forgiving us for the abuse that we have suffered and dealt' does not.

In the same way, there is a need and opportunity to articulate (and, of course, demonstrate) what the Christian faith has to say about our destiny and purpose, about the design, order and awesomeness of creation, about God and the spiritual realm, and about suffering and social dislocation, in language that connects with people.

Who is Jesus?

The widely positive attitude to Jesus serves as a reminder that we stray from him at our peril. Even given the fact that, along with every other age, ours has remade Jesus in its own image (the human being, teacher, individual, and rebel, touched by spiritual wisdom, who was persecuted and then misrepresented by the authorities), his power, wisdom and challenge to us still shine through.

That said, he was somewhat enfeebled by being treated as just a 'good teacher', in much the same way as the Bible was neutered by being treated as 'just' a story, a series of metaphors, moral education for children, or some such moderately safe formula.

The need to rehabilitate both to their authentic and challenging roles, by explaining the idea of genre within the Bible, by arguing for the historical reliability of the Gospels, by exploding the 'just a good teacher' myth, and by similar (essentially apologetic) activities is great, not least within congregations themselves!

A vision of heaven

The widespread appeal of the idea of heaven is encouraging, if not difficult to explain. The fact that a paucity of credible visions of heaven meant that that 'appeal' rarely progressed any further than a vague, hesitant, personalised, and almost embarrassed speculation is less encouraging.

There are, of course, dangers attendant on the attempt to outline a vision of heaven, not least because the Bible is neither particularly clear not particularly interested in the topic. Yet, the long history of Christian visions (see, for example, Alister McGrath's *A brief history of heaven*) encourages careful and humble speculation, and may be used as a point by means of which people's values can be assessed and explored. People's vision of heaven naturally reflects their own concerns and interests and encouraging them to describe that vision provides a constructive means of exploring what they value in life and how they would wish to see those values perfected. The fact that, at least according to *Beyond the Fringe* respondents, good, personal relationships are named as the most important factor in their lives and are commonly the centre-piece of their vision of heaven, is another contact point for a faith that is, at heart, about relationships.

The values of research

Although *Beyond the Fringe* respondents came from a range of backgrounds, life stages and socio-economic groups, and may be taken as reasonably typical of those outside the Christian fold today, it is always dangerous generalising from small samples. Their interviews, in as far as they covered shared ground, confirmed the findings of other studies. Nevertheless particular parishes will have particular conditions that shape opinions and attitudes in the area and, for that reason, further research is always useful. Conducting similar studies in their own area may help congregations connect with people they would not normally meet, and understand if and what particularities exist in their parish.

This is not necessarily the only value of conducting research, however. One of the commonest responses among those interviewed was an expression of how pleased they were to have an opportunity to talk about matters that were usually buried under the practical demands of their busy lives. The very act of listening to people in this way models a community that offers stillness, depth and an opportunity for people to explore their spiritual thoughts without fear of judgement.

Moreover, this is an opportunity that is increasingly rare in our frenetic, 24/7, media-saturated, entertainment-driven, consumer culture. The fact that all respondents had big questions that they wanted answering was often buried under the concerns of everyday life or, if they were painful questions, anaesthetised by omnipresent entertainment and sophisticated encouragements to feel better by spending more money. Not only might churches fruitfully provide a forum in which people can operate as human beings rather than as consumers, but by offering the opportunity to reflect on these key areas of life. Either through actual research or in some less formal conversational format, they can encourage this powerful, motivating but often suppressed aspect of people's nature. Even those respondents who professed atheistic, materialist nihilism valued the opportunity to talk about the big life questions they had.

The lens of relationships

Relational thinking is probably the strongest single contact point between those in and out of the Christian fold. Relationships are a human fundamental, of interest and importance to all, commonly central to tentative visions of heaven, and often, in their dysfunctional form, at the heart of people's social concerns.

They are also central to the Christian story. The vision at the start of the biblical narrative is of man, woman and the rest of creation relating to one another and to their creator in a harmonious and fulfilling way. The subsequent 'fall' ruptures these relationships, marking them with disobedience, fear, blame, toil, and pain. The resolution of the rupture comes in the incarnation, when God and man are fused in Jesus of Nazareth, whose life and work was to heal relationships and re-incorporate wholeness or shalom into creation. The narrative ends with a vision of a city in which creation and creator live and rejoice together in right relationship. From beginning to end, relationships dominate the Christian story.

Right relationships are made possible through the self-emptying love that Christ demonstrated in his life and teachings. Love is the object of life, the goal of creation and the foundation of the moral order. Human beings are here to 'love the Lord […] with all your heart […] soul […] mind and […] strength [and] love your neighbour as yourself.' The incarnation, crucifixion and resurrection reveal and restore the created order of love, 'making all things new.'

This focus on love and relationships will not only make instinctive sense to many outside the Christian tradition but also connect naturally with their values and vocabulary. By embodying a community that models right relationships between people, by encouraging an 'environmental' outlook that seeks to mend the relationship between people and the rest of creation, and by retelling and enacting a story that describes the healing of the relationship between humanity and its creator, and inviting others to participate in that story, the Church today can reach out to an enormous fringe constituency which is determinedly 'irreligious' but self-consciously spiritual.

Moving on

This research project provides the background for and needs to be read in the context of the various publications and resources outlined in the Accompanying Resources section (page 10). The books – *Evangelism in a Spiritual Age: communicating faith in a changing culture* and *Equipping Your Church in a Spiritual Age* – attempt to provide a more detailed, practical response to these and many other issues raised in this report.

Evangelistic contact cards, posters and follow-up materials, produced by The Christian Enquiry Agency provide a further resource, as does the website www.churchinaspiritual age.org.uk, which has been set up to provide information, ideas and links for all those wishing to pursue the issues further.

Beyond the Fringe: Researching a Spiritual Age confirmed and filled in the details of the thesis that originally led Yvonne Richmond to instigate the project. There is an interesting, vibrant and growing spirituality among those outside the church. In spite of varying degrees of resistance and hostility among some people, there is real opportunity for Christians to connect with this spiritual age in faithful, motivating and inspiring ways.